PRODUCT
DESIGN MODELS

PRODUCT
DESIGN MODELS

Roberto Lucci   **Paolo Orlandini**

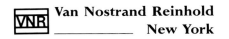
Van Nostrand Reinhold
New York

Copyright © 1990 by Van Nostrand Reinhold

Library of Congress Catalog Card Number 88-34844

ISBN 0-442-20654-2

Printed in the United States of America

Designed by Keano Design Studio

Van Nostrand Reinhold
115 Fifth Avenue
New York, New York 10003

Van Nostrand Reinhold International Company Limited
11 New Fetter Lane
London EC4P 4EE, England

Van Nostrand Reinhold
480 La Trobe Street
Melbourne, Victoria 3000, Australia

Nelson Canada
1120 Birchmount Road
Scarborough, Ontario M1K 5G4, Canada

16 15 14 13 12 11 10 9 8 7 6 5 4 3 2 1

Library of Congress Cataloging-in-Publication Data

Lucci, Roberto.
  Design models / Roberto Lucci, Paolo Orlandini.
    p.   cm.
  Includes index.
  ISBN 0-442-20654-2
  1. Architectural models. 2. Engineering models.
I. Orlandini, Paolo. II. Title.
NA2790.L83 1989
720′.228—dc19   88-34844
                              CIP

Contents

Foreword

Before initiating their brilliant professional careers, Roberto Lucci and Paolo Orlandini were qualified collaborators in my office in the years 1965–74. During that period I discovered their commitment and vivacious creativity, qualities rarely found so well coordinated and integrated in two designers who work and teach together.

This useful book will become essential as an introduction to simple techniques of model-making. It will certainly become a basic text on how best to develop a project to its most critical phase—the transformation from the concept to the three-dimensional object, and then to the production prototype. Distinct among the various techniques of representation, the construction of three-dimensional models widens the range of the design control and presents itself as a rich design tool.

The model is a valuable aid in avoiding the risk of abstraction in projects finalized only with regard to their form. From the very beginning of the design process the model relates to the problems of manufacturing. Frequently during the construction of the model, the designer gains insights into the technical experience that suggest valid solutions to problems in all production areas.

This book is consistent with the design approach of Lucci and Orlandini, who are accustomed to working on familiar terms with the materials and to being guided by those materials to their final form. This love and feeling for the materials from the very beginning of the creative process is a very Italian tradition. To be guided by the material is a way of interpreting reality while acquiring more experience.

Model-making also has significant educational implications. The basis of this representational tool is the need to communicate: to oneself, to verify one's own idea; to others, in order to make one's idea known and understood. Once brought into the classroom, this function becomes an effective teaching instrument. Here students become accustomed to controlling and critiquing their ideas and simultaneously developing a professional attitude toward communication. This method is by far more effective for describing a project than verbal explanation can be.

It must be clear that model-making is a tool to be used together with an appropriate system of control. This prevents the model from becoming an end in itself, under the false pretense of being the final project. Naturally this depends on how the discipline is presented to students. If it is approached without an adequately rigorous methodology, such as is customary with other techniques of representation, model-making risks becoming merely a formal exercise without achieving its purpose.

It is worth recalling that historically, in the schools of sound rationalist tradition, the model served only as a basic check. It was used to evaluate the mass, the proportion, the composition as well as other relatively abstract aspects of the project, without the ties of realistic representation. On this level of abstract representation, model-building played a role in the preliminary instruction of design students.

Another important function of model building is the acquaintance with the technology, intended as a support for the language that governs the shaping of the object. It is obvious that such a function is more effectively expressed in three dimensions than in a two-dimensional drawing.

Model-building, especially the particular method developed by Lucci and Orlandini and illustrated in this book, finds its most efficient application in the conceptual phase of design, when quick and timely verifications lead to the individualization and consolidation of avenues of design.

Marco Zanuso

Preface

This book deals with an original approach to model-making. The methods described in the book represent not only a quick and easy way to build design models but also a means of developing the design process by "sketching" in three dimensions and, at the same time, checking form and structure. Paper, foam, wood, metal, plastic, fabric, rubber, and found objects are the basic materials included in this book. The techniques for working with these materials are not classical ones, but have been especially adapted to this way of model-making.

We believe that the model is a medium for the designer, not the goal. The energy required for building models should, therefore, be minimal in order to encourage the use of this powerful agent in the design process. We teach this with a minimum of equipment, a minimum of material, and a minimum of time. The model becomes then a real tool that can be used, altered, and ultimately discarded without concern for the time and energy spent on its construction. Nonetheless, the result can be so good that often it is suitable as a presentation model. The quality of the results depends far less on the equipment employed or cost of the materials as it does on the attention paid to making a good-looking model.

We are very grateful to Victoria Ogley, whose intelligent help has been an important contribution in the writing of this book. We also wish to thank Debra C. K. Haddock, who provided the English translation of the Foreword.

Introduction

DESIGNING THROUGH MODEL-MAKING

Our way of making models, the result of over twenty years of experience in designing and teaching, is, in a very real sense, a design philosophy. In our view, model-making is a way to design, an activity deeply integrated into the creative process. As a consequence, the drawing is not very important; often it is just a quick early step in the task of making a model. Thus, we do not translate our design ideas from two dimensions into three dimensions; rather, we try to think from the outset in a three-dimensional way. All the quick and easy techniques shown in this book are derived from the basic assumption that model-making is the way we design.

Traditional model-making will probably become obsolete, and the future is easy to forecast: CAS/CAD/CAM. Computerized systems that make it possible to go from the sketch to the model through a computer-controlled milling machine will become the standard. A computerized model-making process is already being used in some of the larger design offices.

The model-making techniques described in this book, however, cannot be easily performed by a computer. For one thing, our techniques mix design and model-making and often bypass the drawing stage. It is still impossible to use a computer to create a three-dimensional object without a specific program. A second reason is it is difficult for a computer-driven machine to build a model made of more than one material (e.g., paper and wire). We are not against computers, but we feel that the "energy-saving" option described in this book will probably remain a human "art" for a long time.

CHOOSING MATERIALS

Traditional design models are made either in clay or from a solid block of wood. More refined models are often vacuum formed in plastic or molded in glass-reinforced polyester. All these techniques are time-consuming and sometimes very expensive. Shaping a solid piece of wood requires heavy equipment, specialized tools, and experience. The finishing job is endless: sanding, filling and sanding again, coating with sealer or primer, painting, and polishing. Clay is messy, difficult to find in many countries and, because it is not a structural material, hard to control. Plastic and polyester models require not only a similar amount of time but also more equipment and money. This often means that once the model is made, the designer is reluctant to make changes, although they may be necessary.

Paper and cardboard, on the other hand, are easy to find, transport, and work with. The tools required are simple and not very expensive. There is no need for a specialized workshop. Almost all of our models were built on a small cutting mat that can be placed on any desk.

Paper is available in a wide range of colors and surface textures. It is a finished material, which means no sanding, painting, or other finishing job is required. It is also an incredibly versatile medium; the possibilities for designing with paper are unlimited. Paper can be shaped to make light objects, such as origami figures, kites, mobiles, or heavy ones, such as packaging and furniture. It even can be used to build large structures; Buckminster Fuller built forty-foot-diameter domes out of corrugated paper.

Paper resembles sheet metal in that it is thin but strong. A simple fold will turn paper into a structural material. Its properties often pinpoint the structural limitations of the design. In that way, it acts not only as a guide but also as a stimulant for realizing new ideas.

Paper is ideal for models that are essentially three-dimensional sketches, or check models. In most cases it is the quickest medium to work with. It can be cut easily with scissors and quickly glued; whereas with other materials, whether precision work is required or not, time-consuming cutting tools and adhesives must be used.

Despite paper's many qualities, it is not always possible to use it or to use it for all parts of the model.

Other materials that satisfy the requirements of low cost, little time, little material, and little effort include foams (expanded resins); wood and plastic dowels and sheets; metal sheets, tubing, and wire; rubber; fabric; and even found objects. All are easy to find, light and easy to handle, and easy to work with. They are also relatively inexpensive and require only modest equipment.

Foam, in particular, is becoming a favorite among designers. The nice thing about foam is that it allows the designer to make forms—such as large, solid shapes—that would, if made of wood or clay, require heavy equipment and a lot of time.

CONSIDER SCALE

There is a strict relationship between choice of material and scale of the model. For that reason, material and scale should be decided upon at the same time.

Wooden or plastic dowels are well suited for building most scale models, unless the true object is a very small item. Paper is not recommended for large models because, even with an internal frame, it will eventually warp. Hard foams, on the contrary, work well for large models.

It is advisable, whenever possible, to work in scale, because the reduction in size creates a better understanding of the overall shape of the new design. As Claude Lévi-Strauss says in his book *La Pensée Sauvage* (1962) "... the model's intrinsic value is that it compensates for the giving up of actual dimensions with the acquisition of comprehensible dimensions."

When selecting a scale to work in, the designer should weigh several factors. Working in small scale can save time and material, but a model built in a very small scale will loose its details. The 1:10 scale could be appropriate for a model of a kitchen but it would be too small for a chair, when it is important to see the details. It is possible to save time *and* preserve details by building a simple scale model of the overall design and a full-size model of an important detail.

At the other end of the spectrum, a scale of 1:2 can often be deceiving. Instead of understanding that the model is built in scale, the observer may interpret it as representing a full-scale small object.

It once happened to us that the 1:2 scale model of an air-conditioning unit was misunderstood by our client as an achievement in the reduction of the unit's entire mechanism. He was disappointed when he realized that he was only looking at a scale model!

CONSIDER SHAPE

When choosing the material, it is important to try to visualize the shape of the model; surprisingly, this can be done better mentally than by drawing. Because many elements of the design are not complete in the designer's mind at this early stage in the design process, the designer need only imagine a rough shape and some meaningful details, such as radiuses or functional parts (knobs, handles). These are important elements when considering the material with which to build a model.

A boxlike shape with sharp corners and a lot of graphics, knobs, buttons, or the like, for example, should be made out of paper. The details can be realized with found objects or by following the hints explained in the discussion of Special Effects in Chapter 1. If the design will have many radiuses, spherical corners, or soft round shapes, foams are better suited than paper. If the model will be covered with graphics, however, be aware that it is quite difficult to apply graphics to porous materials like foams. Scale models of chairs or tables can be made out of a combination of plastic rods and paper, if the design will have bent tubing; or wood sheets and sticks, if the design is linear.

CONSIDER COLOR

Another consideration regards the final look of the model; the color and the finish of the model should be chosen appropriately at the outset. It will save time to choose a material with a finished surface in the color or colors desired. Alternatively, the surfaces can be covered or painted.

The black-and-white option has advantages in presentation models; whereas using color is always a delicate problem, more so than ever when presenting a new design to a client.

Some colors may cause adverse psychological reactions (for example, some people simply do not like yellow, others hate violet). With a colored model there is always the risk that the design will be refused just because of the color. White, black, and gray are not considered real colors, so their influence on the evaluation of the model will be limited. Furthermore, they are easy colors to match, which saves time, effort, and materials.

CONSIDER PURPOSE

The purpose of the model is another important factor to consider when selecting the material.

Paper is preferred for sketch, or check, models, but good-looking presentation models also can be made out of paper when more time and precision are devoted to the project. In general, however, presentation models are best made with a combination of materials (paper and wood, or wood and plastic, foam and paper). This ensures that the design is not affected by the limitations of a single material.

CONSIDER REALISM

How realistic a model should be depends on many different factors, chief among them the purpose of the model, choice of materials, and the amount of time available.

The first thing to consider is the purpose of the model. It is obvious that a presentation model requires more realism than a design process model that will never go out of the office. Nonetheless, some clients may be able to understand the symbolic aspects of a model that expresses the qualities of the design without strictly adhering to realistic features.

Materials have a direct relationship to realism. Extremely realistic models can be constructed from paper, so long as spherical forms are not involved. Wood, metal, and plastic lend themselves well to realism. On the other hand, it is almost impossible to make truly realistic models out of foam, although foam models that effectively communicate the spirit of the design may be appropriate for certain clients.

Striving for realism above all other values can consume an unjustifiable amount of time. If a realistic presentation model requires more time than is available, some realism may have to be sacrificed in favor of such other characteristics as freshness of the materials and cleanliness of execution. Both are very important in achieving an elegant model. Paper is usually a good option in such cases.

Once decisions have been made about materials, scale, and degree of realism, it is best to stick to them until the model is finished. Changes of mind in any phase of the model-building process generally lead to failure. Switching materials or scale, or trying to incorporate more or less realism once building has begun, usually results in a lot of extra work and a poorly constructed model.

If you realize that you have selected the wrong material or that the scale is either too big or too small, do not switch in midstream. Either stop and throw away what you have done up to that point or finish the model as originally conceived and then make a new one taking advantage of the experience gained from making the first.

In the pages that follow, we will explore the materials and techniques for making design process and presentation models that most effectively exhibit the intended concept at the same time as they aid in the creative process and save time, materials, and effort. The extensive examples offered in Part II are intended to illustrate the relationship between design and model-making, showing how our design ideas were converted into models. Many examples also show how the design process evolved through the models.

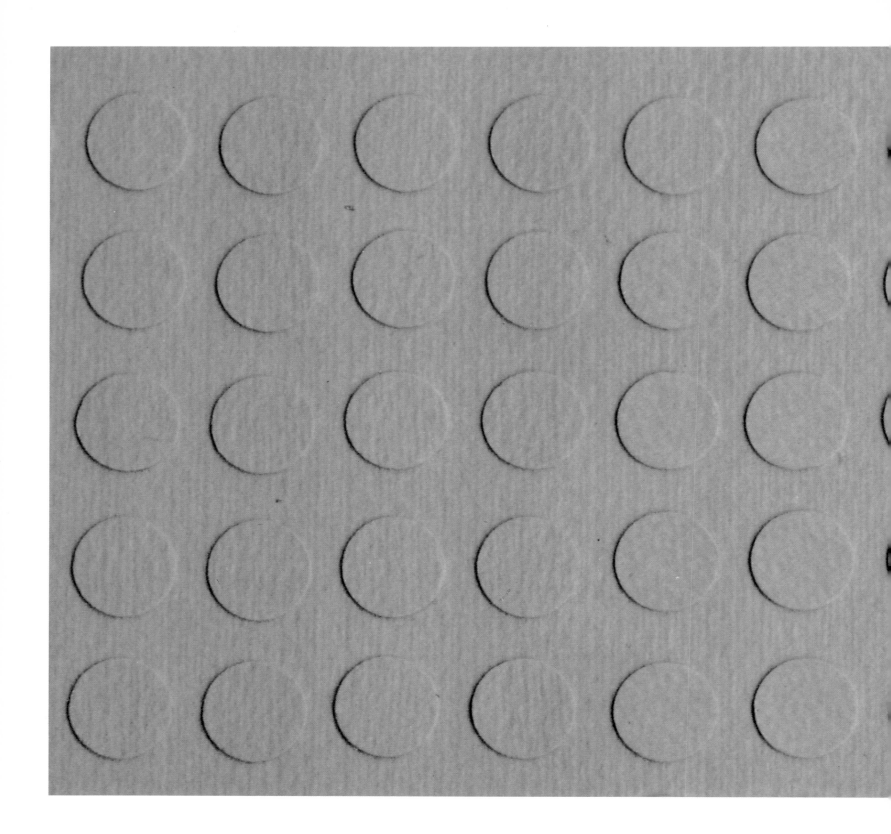

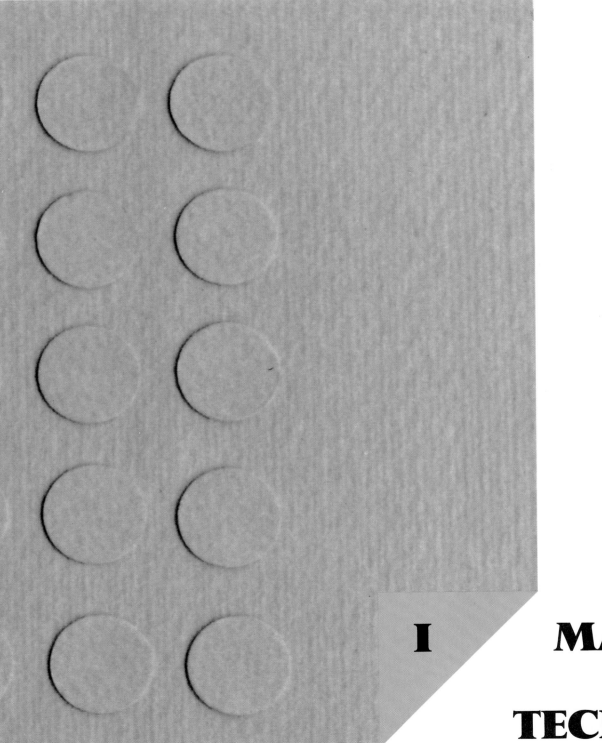

I

MATERIALS AND TECHNIQUES

1 ▨▨▨ PAPER AND BOARDS

A huge variety of papers and boards is available today, but for our models we generally use only a few types. Brand names vary in different countries, and we have given only a few examples, but any paper or board with similar characteristics (weight, surface texture, color) can be used.

MATERIALS

PAPER

One-ply paper ($\frac{1}{100}$ inch; 0.25mm; 120–150 g/m^2)—for finishing jobs; for very small models, including check models. Examples: Canson Mi-Teintes has a vellum surface and is available in a variety of soft colors; ideal for covering, bends very easily. Strathmore drawing paper, available in smooth or slightly grainy surface, usually only in white; also excellent for covering, bends easily.

Two-ply paper ($\frac{1}{80}$ inch; 0.32mm; 240 g/m^2)—for small models, quick check models, and models with bent surfaces. Examples: Bristol, available from many manufacturers in medium and smooth surfaces; bright white; its stiff yet thin quality makes it the best material for covering medium-sized structures; bends well. Two-ply cover stock, available in many colors, matte finish; although not as stiff as Bristol, it can be used similarly.

Three-ply paper ($\frac{1}{64}$ inch; 0.4mm; 300–360 g/m^2)—heavy paper; for most paper models. Example: single-thick cover stock, construction paper; available in matte finish and many colors; suitable for almost any model.

Four-ply paper ($\frac{1}{40}$ inch; 0.6mm; 400–480 g/m^2)—very heavy paper, for medium and large models requiring little or no bending. Examples: double-thick cover stock, available in black, white, and occasionally colors; smooth or vellum finish; as a structural and, at the same time, a finished material, it is best suited for fairly large flat surfaces (up to 8 by 8 inches/200 × 200mm); quite hard to bend, particularly in radiuses of less than ¾ inch (20mm).

Glossy paper (two- and three-ply)—for use when a glossy exterior is required; for finishing jobs only. Examples: Dura-Glo, Chromolux coated cover stock, easily scratched, requires a great deal of attention when being glued. The vapors from solvent glues and contact cement pass through the paper and spoil the surface. Spray adhesive or white glue, applied in very thin layers, is best for this paper. Edges are generally white, since the support for the glossy sheet is white paper; color edges with a marker to match surface color (Fig. 1-1).

BOARD

Cardboard ($\frac{1}{32}$–$\frac{1}{16}$ inch; 0.8–1.6mm; 500–1000 g/m²)—for all structural parts and large flat surfaces of a model; not recommended for curved parts with radiuses smaller than 2½ inches (65mm). Examples: Chipboard; does not have a finished surface so is suitable only for structural parts that will later be covered. Illustration board, very heavy Bristol board; both have finished surfaces.

Corrugated board—particularly well-suited for large structural mock-ups, permitting a quick view of the rough form, size, proportions, and structure of model; not suitable for precision models since cutting through open grooves results in uneven cut; surfaces are rough and porous, requiring care when glued; unfinished surfaces require painting or covering. (See Chapter 10 for use of corrugated board in storage and shipping of models.) Available in three thicknesses: single-faced (⅛ inch/3.2mm), very flexible, useful for building inner structures of cylindrical shapes; double-faced (⅛ inch/3.2mm), good for interior structures of large models and mock-ups, though its tendency to warp makes it unsuitable for large flat surfaces; triple-faced (⅓ inch/ 8.5mm), generally made from a single-faced and double-faced laminated together, sturdier and less likely to warp than double-faced, suited for structure of very large models, mock-ups, children's toys, and full-sized furniture (Fig. 1-2).

1-1. A selection of papers (top to bottom): glossy two-ply; four-ply; three-ply; two-ply; one-ply.

1-2. Cardboard (chipboard and very heavy Bristol) (lower left); foamcore (right); single-faced corrugated paper, double-, and triple-faced corrugated board (upper left).

FOAMCORE

The more we work with this versatile material, the more we discover its potential. Available in several thicknesses, the most common foamcore (³/₁₆ inch/5mm) is a sheet of polystyrene or polyurethane foam sandwiched between smooth white paperboard facings. The polystyrene has some tendency to warp; the polyurethane is covered with heavier paper, is sturdier and less likely to warp, but is more expensive and less widely available.

Foamcore is particularly good for building quick models, structural mock-ups, and the inside structure of medium-to-large models. Light yet sturdy, it can be used to check the structure and mechanics of a model, even in a 1:1 scale. Soft to cut, easy to mark and work with, it is superior to corrugated board when precision is required. With care and proper techniques, it even can be used to make curved forms.

TOOLS

KNIVES

Among the many utility knives available on the market, we recommend the following as basic tools for cutting paper, boards, and other similar materials. They perform different jobs, from tough to very delicate work, and offer different degrees of precision. All have replaceable blades so it is easy to maintain a sharp edge, essential for accurate cutting (Fig. 1-3).

Mat knife—for cutting cardboard, corrugated board, and other heavy materials. We prefer a knife with a nonretractable blade, such as that made by Stanley, because it is simple and sturdy and replacement blades are widely available. Its large handle withstands a lot of pressure during heavy cutting jobs. Stanley makes accessories, including a saw blade, that can be attached to the handle.

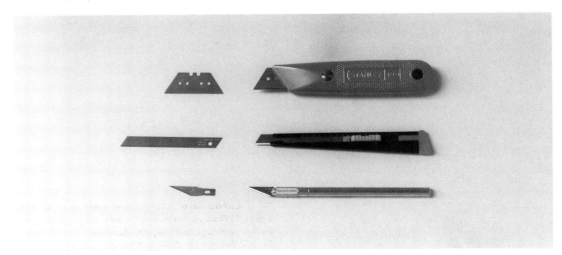

1-3. Basic knives (top to bottom): Stanley mat knife, Olfa model 180 snap-off knife, and X-Acto no. 1 with pointed blade.

Snap-off knife—a general-purpose knife good for most light cutting jobs. This handy knife has a built-in blade snapper, which provides a sharp edge without the need to change blades. Look for a knife, such as the Olfa model 180, with a metal or metal-reinforced handle; an all-plastic handle will twist under pressure.

X-Acto no. 1—the classic versatile knife for precision work. A large selection of interchangeable blades is available to suit the job. The pointed blade (no. 11) that usually comes with the basic aluminum handle is good for cutting adhesive films, cutting into small areas, and detail work.

SCISSORS

Only two types of scissors are essential in model-making (Fig. 1-4).

Straight-blade scissors—for cutting medium to large items; often used when making rough models and for cutting large circles. Asymmetrical handles (such as those on Fiskars) keep the hand out of the way of the paper while cutting. Do not use scissors to cut cardboard; the cut will not be clean and the blades will become blunt.

Curved-blade nail scissors—for cutting small pieces and details with round shapes; circles with diameters of $^{11}\!/_{16}$ inch (18mm) or more; round holes with diameters of $^3\!/_8$ inches (35mm) or more; do not use for cutting holes on paper thicker than three-ply or for straight lines. Buy high-quality nail scissors, because the points of cheap ones will bend when cutting heavy paper.

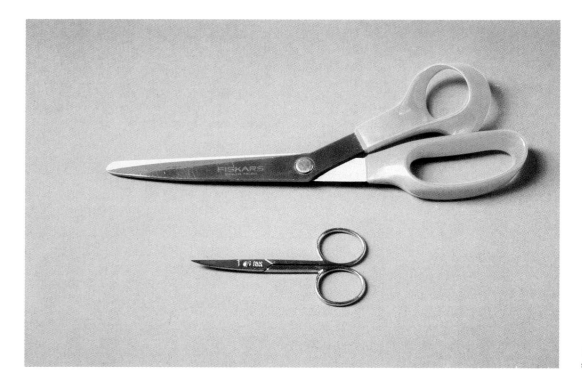

1-4. Scissors (top to bottom): Fiskars straight-blade scissors and nail scissors.

TOOLS FOR CUTTING CIRCULAR SHAPES

Hollow punch—for holes and circles in diameters from $^{2}/_{16}$ to $^{9}/_{16}$ inch (3–14mm). Punches are available with larger diameters but they require a great amount of pressure to cut through the paper. The punch must be very sharp, otherwise the hole (or circle) will have an uneven rim. Note that even new punches may not always be sharp enough. Sharpen with 400-grit waterproof abrasive paper. Roll a small piece into a tube with the abrasive surface on the outside and stick it halfway inside the punch. Turn the punch around the abrasive paper until the inside edge has reached the desired sharpness. Then sharpen the outside edge by rolling the paper into a tube, abrasive side in, and turning the paper around the punch.

Hollow punches are fast and accurate tools. Of course, a different punch is needed for each size hole. Usually, however, hollow punches are not very expensive tools. They perform precise jobs and are quick to use, but only for holes between $^{2}/_{16}$ and $^{9}/_{16}$ inches in diameter (Fig. 1-5).

Compass blade attachment—for diameters over $^{9}/_{16}$ inch (14mm). If such an attachment is not available a sharpened compass point will do. Sharpen the point on a small sheet of 400-grit waterproof abrasive paper or a sharpening stone. A compass will leave a hole in the center of the circle.

Circle cutter—for diameters between $^{11}/_{16}$ and $6^{3}/_{4}$ inches (18–170mm); creates circles without marking the center of the circle; it produces holes and circles at the same time and can be used to make rings of various widths. Expensive and possibly difficult to find in your locality, a circle cutter nonetheless is a handy and accurate cutting tool (Fig. 1-6).

STRAIGHTEDGE

Always buy the heaviest rulers and triangles. Metal is preferred over plastic, which chips when used as a cutting guide. To avoid slippage when pressure is applied during cutting, look for cork or rubber backings. Alternatively, a nonslip backing can be made by using double-coated adhesive tape to attach a piece of rubber, cork, or abrasive paper to the underside of the ruler or triangle.

CUTTING MAT

Never cut directly on your table or other unprotected surface, as it will be permanently damaged even with minimal pressure applied. Several options are available as portable cutting surfaces, some more suitable than others (Fig. 1-7).

Masonite—inexpensive, but must be replaced often because blades cut into it very easily. If not replaced frequently the old cuts will misguide the knife when cutting. In addition, Masonite dulls blades.

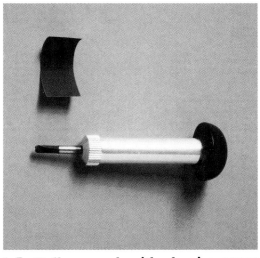

1-5. Hollow punch with abrasive paper rolled inside it.

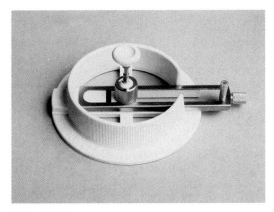

1-6. Circle cutter.

1-7. Aluminum ruler and triangle. Cutting mats (left to right): glass, Masonite, Uchida semihard plastic.

Semihard plastic—excellent permanent cutting base with resilient surface that allows smooth, precise, nonslip cutting. Under normal pressure the cut "heals" instantly. Glued material holds to the mat but peels off easily. The Uchida mat usually comes with time-saving grid guidelines. Should not be used with the hollow punch, which will permanently damage the surface.

Glass—durable surface, but breakable and quickly wears down the knife blade.

Unsuitable materials include plywood, which will chip after a while, and Formica, which produces an abrasive sand.

SCORING TOOLS

In order to bend paper it is necessary first to score it. Many types of scoring tools are available; choose according to the radius of the bend. (See How to Score for Bending in this chapter.)

Compass point—plastic or metal handle to which the compass point can be attached usually comes with the compass kit. When scoring, hold it at an angle; held perpendicularly it will scratch the surface to be scored.

Awl—like the compass point, it should not be held perpendicular to the surface to be scored.

Other good scoring tools include old **ballpoint pens** (empty of any ink), **aluminum knitting needles,** and **metal burnishers** (Fig. 1-8).

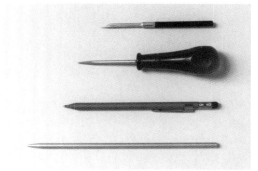

1-8. Scoring tools (top to bottom): compass point, awl, ballpoint pen, aluminum knitting needle.

HOLDING AND CLAMPING TOOLS

A variety of items should be kept handy for clamping and holding together sections of the model during the gluing process. Assembling a stock ahead of time will permit you to select the appropriate clamp, pin, or whatever depending on the shape, side, or corner being glued.

The appropriate tool depends on the size and the shape of the model being built and on the material being used. Avoid holding parts of the model together with your hands while waiting for the glue to dry. Hands are never steady enough and can stain the paper.

Among those tools and devices we have found useful are (Fig. 1-9):

- **Clothes pins**—the tips of wooden ones can be modified to suit shape of model.
- **Hair clips** (coiffure clips)—metal or plastic.
- **Pins**—straight pins, ball pins, push pins, map tacks.
- **Paper clips**
- **Paper clamps**
- **C-clamps**—small sizes.
- **Tweezers**—straight or curved tips.
- **Miscellaneous:** books, iron, hammer; for weighing down pieces that have just been glued.

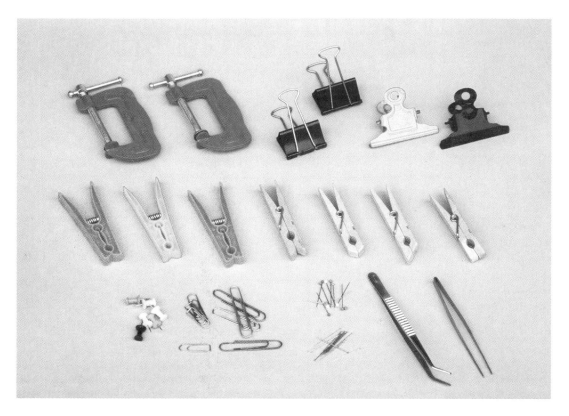

1-9. Holding and clamping devices (top to bottom, left to right): C-clamps, paper clamps, clothes pins, push pins, paper clips, straight pins, pins, tweezers.

ADHESIVES

Adhesives include glues, cements, and tapes. The adhesive chosen depends in part on the material on which it is used. Drying time, color and finish when dried, and the effect an adhesive has on the model material are other considerations. In general, it is a good idea to test any glue and material combination you have never worked with before to see if damage to color or surface occurs (Fig. 1-10).

GLUES

White glue—a good all-purpose glue that can be used for most jobs; the one we use the most. It is clean, dries clear, and is not shiny, an important feature when working with paper, which almost always has a matte surface. The many other high-performance glues dry either too quickly or too slowly and tend to be messy.

White glue is an emulsion of copolymerpolyvinyl acetate resin and water. As a water-based glue it has to be used with caution on paper. See discussion of Gluing in this chapter.

Glue stick—useful with papers thinner than two-ply when a strong joint is not needed; does not wrinkle thin paper like liquid white glue does. Because the stick is

1-10. An international selection of glues for paper: balsa cements (lower left); rubber cements and spray adhesive (upper left); white glues (upper right); glue sticks (lower right).

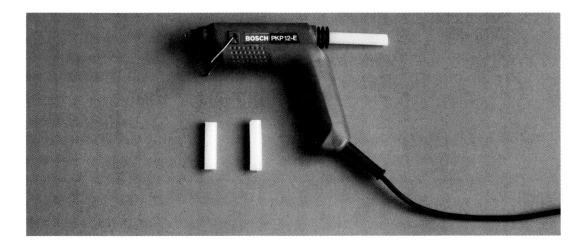

wide, it is good for gluing wide surfaces of thin paper; it is awkward to use for small areas, however, because the spread of the glue is impossible to control.

Glue gun—excellent for structural jobs, especially for gluing large sheets of foam-core or corrugated board. Solid glue sticks are heated to melting point inside the gun, then dispensed through a nozzle. Glue dries instantly, thus no clamping is necessary and resulting joints are very strong. Refills are available in different qualities and strengths, providing elastic or rigid joints. Glue guns can be messy because it is hard to control the quantity of glue that comes out; we suggest using them only for structural parts that will be covered (Fig. 1-11).

CEMENTS

Balsa cement—good for structural jobs because it dries fast and is strong; can be used on cardboard and thin paper, but not on foamcore (its solvents will melt the foam) or glossy paper (it will mar the glossy coating). Use with caution because it dries shiny, making glue spots noticeable.

Rubber cement—often used for very wide surfaces, for example, when covering a large foamcore form with paper. Easy to use and clean up since excess can be rubbed off. Rubber cement is not structural: It is not strong enough to bond thick pieces of paper or board bent to form a narrow radius, and elements glued together under continuous tension will eventually separate. Nor is it permanent: As it oxidizes it loses its adhesive power, and after one or two years pieces of the model will begin to peel off. (See Matte acetate tape in this chapter for a solution to this problem.) Solvent will stain colored papers and mar glossy surfaces.

Spray adhesive—useful in situations similar to those suitable for rubber cement and has the same limitations of structural strength and permanence. Faster and easier to use than rubber cement, but messier; it is essential to mask all areas not to be glued before spraying. Safer than rubber cement with colored or glossy papers, but test before using.

A variety of tapes are available for temporary or permanent assemblage of model elements. As with glues and cements, not all tapes are suitable for all surfaces and weights of paper and board (Figs. 1-12, 1-13, 1-14).

Transparent cellophane—rarely used in model-making; suitable only for temporary jobs, because it eventually yellows and peels off (it oxidizes). Because it is shiny, it should be used only on glossy paper.

Clear polyester—an extremely transparent film tape that is almost invisible on clear acetate and glossy paper; particularly well suited for finished models and precision work; provides a cleaner look than cellophane tape; adheres better and therefore resists oxidation better than cellophane tape. More expensive and less widely available than cellophane tape.

Matte-finish acetate—for example, 3M Magic Transparent tape; almost invisible;

1-12. Single-coated tapes (clockwise from upper left): clear polyester tape, drafting tape, matte-finish acetate tape, transparent cellophane tape.

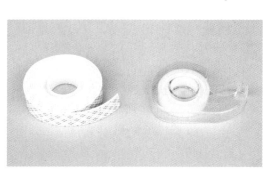

1-13. Double-coated tapes (left to right): foam tape, transparent tape.

1-14. Adhesive foil strips (top) and Letra-line charting tape (bottom).

for use on matte surfaces only. Can be used to add strength and permanence to joints glued with rubber cement or spray adhesive.

Drafting—easily removed without damaging paper; excellent for temporarily taping together a joint while glue is setting. Be sure not to press the tape on strongly, and always peel it off very slowly to guarantee against damaging the surface of the model.

Double-coated transparent—with adhesive on both sides; for taping two surfaces to each other. Often used as an alternative to spray adhesive; like spray adhesive, should not be used for structural joints and bonds under continuous tension, including curved paper, which will try to reassume its original flat shape. Because it has no solvents in it, can be employed without marring the surface of glossy paper. Apply with care to avoid bubbles and wrinkles.

Double-coated foam—too thick to be used for taping paper; better suited for taping cardboard to cardboard and other materials. Creates a very strong joint by filling the gaps and air spaces between two uneven surfaces, thus increasing the contact area.

Charting—Letraline, for example; available in a wide range of colors, widths, and finishes; for graphic details, for representing the space between two parts of an object, like grooves and gaskets. Metal-finish tapes are good for imitating metal and chrome trims.

Flexible crepe—Letraline Flex-A-Tape, for example; a highly flexible tape that can be formed into small or large curves; very useful for tracing curved lines that have a constant width.

ADHESIVE FOIL

1-15. A selection of adhesive foils.

Adhesive foils come in a wide range of colors, textures, and finishes that are impossible to find in paper, including glossy, matte, metal, wood, cork, marble, and cloth. Found in hardware, paint, and wallpaper stores, they can be used to achieve realistic effects in scale models. Cut in strips, they can be used as charting tape is; they should never be used to cover wide areas of paper (Fig. 1-15).

WORKING WITH PAPER

BEFORE YOU BEGIN

Before starting to build a model it is important to consider the model-making strategy. We have already expressed our preference for paper as a medium for building models. For this reason we are starting with paper and have devoted more space to it than to other materials. Many of the following general considerations, however, apply to other model-making materials.

A model made out of paper has the potential to well represent the finished product, but only if care and attention have been applied during the building process. A precisely made model will have a freshness and crispness of line, but a dirty and sloppy model will only look cheap.

Many, but not all, imaginable shapes can be made out of paper. Paper is a symbolic material, not the material out of which the product actually will be made. Since it may be impossible to represent in paper all the details of the design, the designer must make a choice. Some part of the shape, or the radiuses, or the corners must be reinterpreted if they are to be made out of paper. Reinterpreting the design so that the model respects the nature of paper will result in a good-looking model that exploits the qualities of the medium (paper) to the maximum. Another option is to build a model that represents only one or a few of the design's most important concepts, such as its proportions, its modularity, or its mechanism.

The decision of what to represent in the model depends on many factors.

If the model is a three-dimensional sketch, it is just a phase in the design process, a practical model that serves for checking the overall shape or the structure. If, on the other hand, it is a presentation model, it must show meaningful design elements. The focus might be on some aesthetic aspect (a large dial, a grille, a large plane, or a curve characterizing the whole shape, as examples). If the purpose of the model is to stress functional features of the design (ease of transportation, visibility, simple assembly, perhaps), simplification may be achieved by stressing one of those features over other aspects of form.

If such simplification is impossible or threatens to negatively influence evaluation of the design, the solution may be to build two models: one, the aesthetic model, and it can even be a scale model; the other one, the functional model. Each can be built in the material best suited for expressing the corresponding design ideas.

After deciding which ideas or details to show, the designer must consider whether the model consists of many composite shapes. If so, the model should be divided into simpler subunits or geometric forms. Each can be built separately and then assembled. This process has three advantages:

1. Building simple geometrical forms is easier and faster than building complex ones.
2. If a mistake is made, in either the design or the model, the whole model need not be thrown away.
3. The work time can be organized so that, for example, while one glued piece is drying, another part can be constructed.

Finally, depending on the size of the model, it is important to determine whether it will require an inner structure. Large models should be made out of foamcore or chipboard and then covered with one- or two-ply paper. Small models can be made of two- or three-ply paper, which will provide the supporting structure and the finished covering at the same time. If the model requires a special finish (glossy, chrome), then even small models will need a supporting structure because these papers and foils are too thin to support themselves.

All presentation models, with the exception of very small ones, should be made out of foamcore and then covered with paper. This will ensure precision and the control of both planarities and radiuses of curvature.

FINDING THE GRAIN

Paper is a fibrous material that passes through rollers during its manufacture. This process aligns the cellulose fibers perpendicularly to the axis of the rollers, thus producing a grain to the paper. Achieving a smooth bend, curve, or fold requires that the paper be bent with the grain, not against it.

To discover which way the grain runs bend the paper at a 90-degree angle, but do not crease it; repeat the process perpendicular to the first bend. The bend that wrinkles and creases the paper has gone against the grain (Fig. 1-16).

1-16. Bends made to determine the direction of the paper's grain: bend parallel to (with) the grain (left); bend perpendicular to (against) the grain (right).

TRACING

Although our design method rarely involves technical drawing, we do draw many sketches of the model. Sometimes these sketches are orthogonal views of the model; more frequently they are informal sketches showing the important details, the dimensions, and the development of the curves. Having done this, the next step is to lightly mark the paper with a pencil where cuts and bends will be made. Obviously, mark the side of the paper that will not be visible on the finished model.

CUTTING

Because paper is a finished material care should be taken when cutting not to mar or otherwise compromise the surface.

Choose the appropriate knife and blade for the material to be cut. To get a clean cut and to have good control over the knife, always be sure the blade is very sharp and clean (there should be no glue on it); a dull blade will tear the paper. Be sure to use a straightedge with a nonslip backing (as pressure is applied to the knife, the ruler might otherwise slide away).

From the first time that the knife slices into the paper be sure that the blade is perpendicular to the paper, not inclined away from or toward the straightedge. With thick paper or foamcore, a tilted knife will result in a beveled edge and the cut piece will be one or two millimeters too short or long.

When working with papers thicker than one-ply, cutting always produces a good side and a bad side because the layers of the paper are pressed together and deformed by the pressure of the blade. The bad side is the side touching the cutting board (Fig. 1-17). When cutting out a piece with unequal sides, be sure to cut it so that the bad side will face inward or not be visible when the model is assembled.

Making round holes—For small round holes with diameters of ²⁄₁₆ to ⁹⁄₁₆ inch (3–14mm) use a very sharp hollow punch. Work on a Masonite board protected with two layers of cardboard; glass and semihard plastic will be broken or damaged by the punch. A special effect can be achieved by covering the cutting surface with many layers of loose leaf paper (a newspaper works well): the softer surface produces what looks like drawn holes in sheet metal (Fig. 1-18).

Begin by tracing a circle on the paper slightly larger than the desired size; in this way the punch can be properly centered. Trace very lightly in pencil so that it can be easily erased later; overerasing damages colored paper.

To punch out a hole, twist the punch back and forth while remaining within the marked circle until it twists through the paper. It is possible to punch holes by applying pressure to the punch without twisting, but a lot of strength is required.

The larger the hole, the more force is needed to punch it out. Holes larger than ½ inch (12mm) require considerable pressure and the punch must be hit with a hammer. When hammering, it is particularly important to hold the punch very steadily; if the punch moves under the hammer strike it will produce holes with blurred edges.

After using the punch be sure to remove the paper dot from the end. It will otherwise act as a stopper, preventing the punch from working properly later.

For holes with diameters over ⁹⁄₁₆ inch (14mm) use a blade attachment to a compass or a sharpened compass point. Pass it around repeatedly until the hole has been cut out.

The larger the hole, the more difficult it is to pass the compass over and over while staying within the designated boundary. The center hole becomes enlarged as the compass is turned around many times. As a result the compass is not fixed and the circle or hole is inaccurate. To avoid this, fix a small piece of paper or tape over the center hole.

Holes with diameters over 1⅜ inches (35mm) can be cut out with nail scissors. Before introducing the scissors into the paper, make a small cut with a knife to give the scissors a point to start from without deforming the paper.

Use a circle cutter for circles and holes from ¹¹⁄₁₆ to 6¾ inches (18–170mm). Because circle cutters do not damage the center it is possible to make a perfect hole and also have a perfect circle. They are also very handy tools for cutting rings. The blade must be sharp and a cutting mat must always be used beneath it. It is best to pass the cutter over the required circumference a few times instead of using one heavy turn, because it is difficult to apply heavy pressure evenly.

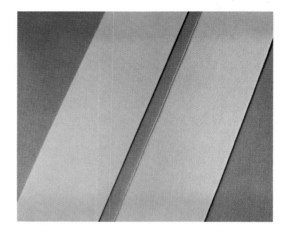

1-17. Good side (left) and bad side (right) of paper that has been cut with a knife.

1-18. Hollow punch and hole sections: punched on Masonite with two layers of cardboard (top); punched on Masonite with newspaper cushioning (bottom).

Making oval, square, rectangular, triangular holes—Noncircular holes are made by tracing the desired shape onto the paper and using a sharp blade to cut it out. If the corners are rounded, use a hollow punch of the appropriate size for the corners, then cut out the straight parts with the knife. Always punch out the rounded corners first; otherwise it will be difficult to place the hole tangent to the straight cut (Fig. 1-19).

If the hole does not have rounded corners, use a compass point to pierce the corners and connect each point by making a straight cut from one angle to the other.

A hole cut with a compass point will have paper fibers extending from it; made with scissors, it will have rough edges. Another imprecision results when the straightedge does not line up perfectly with the rounded corner (in oval or square holes). These imperfections can be sanded away with 400- or 600-grit waterproof abrasive paper; coarser abrasive paper will make the paper hairy.

SCORING

The principle behind scoring is to reduce the thickness of the paper where it will be bent. As with sheet metal, wherever paper is bent it will have a radius; even the sharpest possible bend will have a radius, in that case one that corresponds to the thickness of the paper.

Radiuses of various sizes can be achieved through a combination of the paper thickness, the tool used for scoring, and the work surface used. In general, the thicker the paper and the tool, the wider the radius.

Scoring should always be done on the interior side of the paper, since it reduces the thickness of the paper, spoiling the finished look of the surface.

To make very small radiuses use a compass point for one- to three-ply paper or an awl for one- to four-ply paper. On one-ply paper an awl will produce a slightly larger radius than a compass point will. A compass point should not be used for scoring four-ply paper because it will make too small a groove for such thick paper, thus causing a tear when bent because of tension on the external side.

An empty ballpoint pen produces medium-sized radiuses on one- to three-ply paper; on four-ply paper it forms a small radius, but not as small as that created with an awl. A ballpoint pen is less likely to scratch the paper or nick a straightedge than an awl is. The only drawback is that it may be hard to be certain that the pen is really empty of ink.

Another good scoring tool is an aluminum knitting needle. Never use a plastic knitting needle, which becomes overheated during scoring, leaving traces of plastic on the paper. Knitting needles produce soft bends. Use a knitting needle with a ¼-inch (6mm) shaft or larger. Anything less than ¼ inch is more or less like a ballpoint pen.

The ideal surface on which to score is the semihard plastic cutting mat. For soft radiuses, a rubber or neoprene foam mat is ideal. Wide bends can be achieved by combining a soft work surface with a wide pointed tool and thick paper. When working on a soft surface keep the scoring pressure to a minimum to avoid tearing the paper.

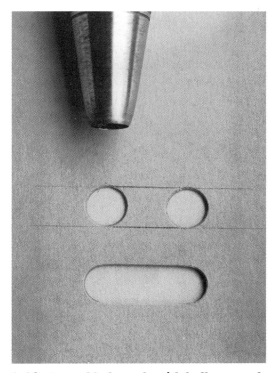

1-19. An oval hole made with hollow punch and knife.

After scoring, it helps to place a ruler or other straightedge in the newly created crease to guide the paper into its new bent shape. The edge of a table can be used for the same purpose (Fig. 1-20).

Bending small pieces of paper risks deforming the paper's extremities, causing the paper to warp slightly (Fig. 1-21). Avoid this by scoring a bigger piece of paper than needed, bending it, and only afterward cutting it down to size.

A similar problem exists when a piece of paper that has a side of ⅜ inch (10mm) or less is bent. It is better to bend a longer piece of paper, then to trim it down to size (Fig. 1-22).

Making narrow radiuses—It is more difficult to make radiuses of ⅛ to ⅜ inch (3 to 10mm) than smaller and larger radiuses. For best results, use paper with a maximum thickness of two-ply and follow these steps:

1. Mark the dimensions of the bend on the paper. Place the paper between two straightedges or rulers; align the rulers along one of the marks and secure the rulers to the paper with C-clamps (Fig. 1-23).
2. With a damp cloth or sponge wipe the inner side of the paper in the area to be bent. Be careful not to spoil the paper with too much water (Fig. 1-24).
3. Hold the paper with two hands and slowly bend it over the top ruler. Change hand positions as you work so that you are holding the paper at different points, not only on the ends or at the center, which will cause it to bow. Take care to apply the same amount of tension to each point (Fig. 1-25).

1-21. The deformed extremity on a small piece of bent paper.

1-20. Bending paper against a table edge after it has been scored.

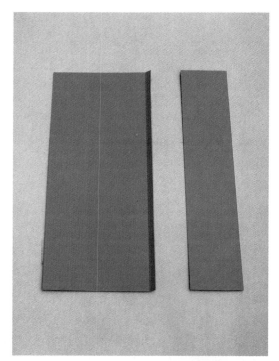

1-22. Bending a piece of paper that must have a narrow side.

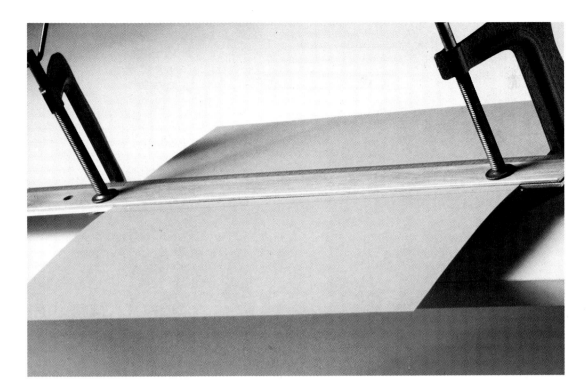

1-23. Bending paper for a radius of $\frac{1}{8}$ to $\frac{3}{8}$ inch (3–10mm). Step 1: Clamping two rulers to the paper.

1-24. Step 2: Moistening the paper with a damp sponge cloth.

An alternative method uses a wooden or plastic dowel of the desired radius to shape the paper. It is more accurate and gives better results than the first method; however it requires the use of a rod that has the exact radius desired, which may not always be on hand. Clamp the paper between two rulers as described above. Place the dowel parallel to the top ruler and slowly bend the paper over the rod. Remember to frequently change hand positions (Fig. 1-26).

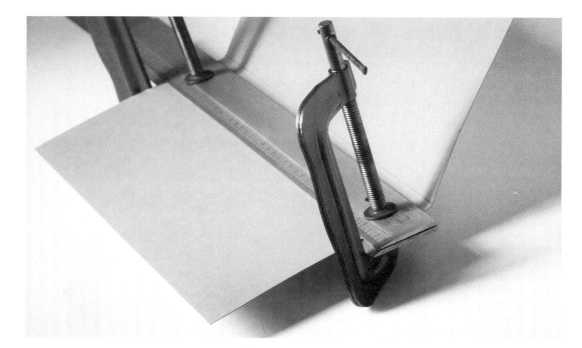

1-25. Step 3: Bending the paper over the top ruler.

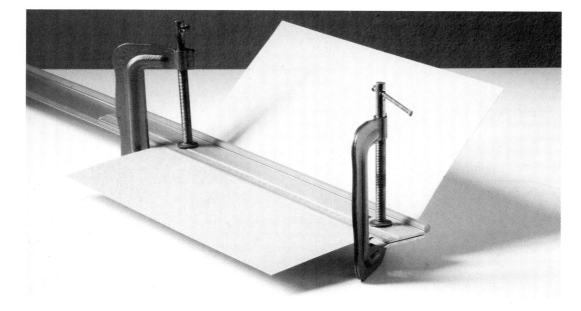

1-26. Alternative method for making a radius of ⅛ to ⅜ inch (3–10mm): Bending the paper over a dowel.

Preshaping wide radiuses—A wide radius, one of ⅜ inch (10mm) or more, is really a curve rather than a bend, and it requires preshaping.

For radiuses from ⅜ to ¾ inch (10–20mm) use one- and two-ply paper; for those over ¾ inch, use three-ply paper. It is possible to use three-ply paper for radiuses under ¾ inch but in such cases preshaping is not advisable. Rather, use the dowel procedure previously described. If it is necessary to curve four-ply paper, the minimum recommended radius is 2 inches (50mm).

To preshape, align the paper with its grain parallel to the edge of a table. Mark on the sheet of paper both ends of the area to be curved. Align one of these two ends to the edge of a table. Taking one edge of the sheet of paper in each hand, pull the paper up and down, rubbing the inside surface of the paper against the table's edge. Be sure to rub up and down only as far as the ends of the area marked for curvature, so that only this area will rub against the table edge. Continue sliding the paper up and down until it becomes curved, or preshaped (Fig. 1-27).

During this process change your hand positions frequently, holding the paper at different points along the top and bottom edges to ensure that the paper will curve evenly. Always apply the same amount of tension to every point along the surface. When preshaping three-ply or four-ply paper, applying too much tension will cause the layers out of which the paper is made to separate. It is important to keep the paper moving back and forth from the moment it is held in tension; if this is not done, the paper will be permanently creased, not curved.

As the paper is slid back and forth, the side touching the table will become worn down and will pick up any dirt on the edge of the table. Colored paper will become

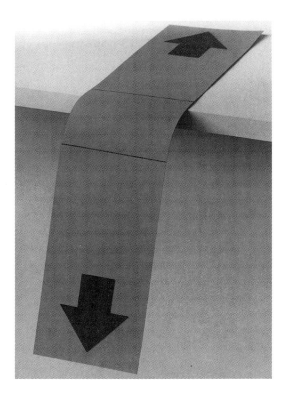

1-27. Preshaping paper using the edge of a table.

shiny. If the paper must be handled a lot to achieve its form, work with a larger piece than needed, then cut it down to size.

Another preshaping technique uses a soft surface and a hard cylindrical form. Because this technique does not spoil the surface of the paper it is particularly useful when the visible part of the curve will be the concave side.

A cloth ironing board cover or a ³/₁₆-inch (5mm) thick sheet of soft polyurethane foam makes a good soft work surface. The hard cylindrical form, which can be a wooden or plastic dowel, is used like a rolling pin. The diameter of the dowel need not correspond exactly to the desired radius, but it should be close to it.

Mark the beginning and end of the curve on the paper. Place the paper on the soft surface and place the dowel parallel to the grain of the paper. Roll the dowel back and forth within the marked area. Apply a lot of pressure but change hand positions frequently to avoid concentrating pressure on one area only (Fig. 1-28).

The preshaped paper will not permanently retain its form without some type of support. For small models support can be provided by bending the edges of the form to create an omega or other similar structural shape and gluing the support to the rest of the model (Fig. 1-29).

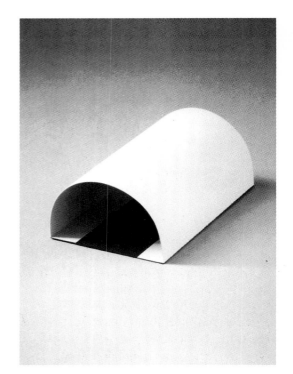

1-29. Gluing a preshaped piece of paper in position to create a structural shape.

1-28. Preshaping paper using a dowel as a rolling pin.

PROVIDING INNER STRUCTURE

Small models with complex curved surfaces or larger models will need an internal support structure. Foamcore is a good material to use for the internal structure of medium to large models. Corrugated board can be used for very large models, but in this case it is advisable to use four-ply paper for the outside, or the covering of the model, to hide the irregular edges of corrugated board.

The internal structure should be made out of a series of parallel bulkheads fixed to a common base. Make sure that all the bulkheads have equal radiuses and that they are aligned parallel to each other. Warping and twisting of the model are the results of poor alignment (Fig. 1-30).

GLUING

Gluing the elements of the model together is a delicate process, particularly when the model has a side 12 inches (300mm) or larger. Although gluing may seem tedious, it is very rewarding since even large shapes can be made without the mess or the tools needed when making models from clay or wood.

Gluing begins with selecting the right adhesive for the job (see Glues earlier in this chapter). Whichever you choose, apply it in small amounts.

When gluing long and wide joints, the best method is to make a row of very small dots on the area to be glued. If they are too big, spread them out with a paper spatula.

Excess glue near edges will ooze out and stain the paper when pressure is applied to the bond. It is difficult to control the flow of glue from a bottle. When gluing very small areas, therefore, it is better to squeeze some glue onto a piece of scrap paper, then take the glue as needed with a toothpick or paper spatula. The toothpick is good for small detail work. The spatula is effective when the joint has already been glued but small areas remain unstuck; the spatula can either be used to put more glue into these spaces or to spread out the glue that is already in the space. Then pressure should be applied to close the joint.

White glue dries relatively slowly; wait at least fifteen minutes before handling a glued element even if it is clamped or weighed down. Balsa cement dries rapidly, so it is necessary to work quickly when using it.

Some models contain a part made from cardboard or foamcore and a curved part made from two- or three-ply paper. As seen when dealing with cardboard, this material is not recommended for curved parts with radiuses smaller than 2½ inches (65mm); the situation is similar for foamcore. Therefore, the problem often arises of joining the two parts (the cardboard or foamcore to the two- or three-ply paper). There will always be a visible line between the curved part and the rest of the model, although skillful gluing can help make the seam inconspicuous. The best strategy is to incorporate the seam into the design so it looks intentional, not accidental.

When gluing the cover to a support structure, apply the glue to the bottom of the model, the corners of bulkheads that are not rounded, and the beginning and end of curved bulkheads (Fig. 1-31). Never apply glue to the top of a bulkhead because it will mark the cover. If it is absolutely necessary to do so in order to attach the cover, it will be necessary to sheathe the cover with a second one, this time applying glue only to the areas previously described.

Apply a lot of very small glue dots at frequent intervals; place extra dots near curved areas where there will be a lot of tension. Glue one side of the structure to the cover and then evenly weigh down the model and give the glue time to dry and set before working on the next side (Figs. 1-32, 1-33, 1-34).

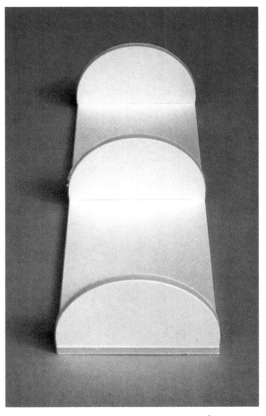

1-30. An internal structure built from foamcore.

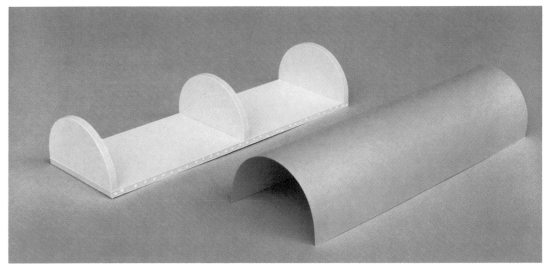

1-31. Applying glue to a foamcore structure. Note that the glue dots are not applied to the bulkheads.

1-32. Glue dots are applied to areas where the paper cover will be under the greatest tension.

1-33, 1-34. Weighing down elements while the glue is drying.

BORDERS AND EDGES

Borders are applied when the model is nearly finished, a point at which there is no room for mistakes. They work as accents, drawing the attention of the eyes, thus it is important to achieve a clean cut and to attach the border neatly and precisely.

Borders can be made out of two- or three-ply paper. One-ply paper is recommended when the border is to be glued to a curved edge. White glue is the best choice of adhesive, especially if the border is glued to a curve with a radius of less than 1 inch (25mm); spray adhesive and rubber cement will lose their elasticity as they oxidize, causing the border to peel off after a while.

Use a spatula to distribute a small amount of glue along the border, making sure to spread glue along the edges. Avoid excess glue, which will ooze out and stain the border and the side surfaces.

Borders for curved edges should be preshaped using the table-edge method described earlier. Since paper has a certain amount of elasticity, it will always try to return to its original shape. It also helps to distribute glue close to the ends of the curve and to apply pressure to the areas on either side of the curve while the glue is drying. In these areas the border is under the most tension and it will try to resume its original shape (Fig. 1-35).

Always cut borders larger than the finished size. Align one side precisely to one edge; trim off the extra paper from the oversized side after the glue has dried. Use a pair of asymmetrical scissors (such as Fiskars) since the handles will not get in the way. Hold the scissors at a forty-five-degree angle. Be careful not to spoil the edge of the model by rubbing the blades of the scissors along it (Fig. 1-36).

If the model can be placed on a cutting mat and a straightedge held against the edge a knife can be used to trim the border. The blade of the knife must be very sharp. Never try to cut freehand with a knife. Although it looks easy, there is the possibility of slicing into or nicking the model.

1-35. The border at left was improperly glued. In the area of the paper's maximum tension the border has become detached from the curve.

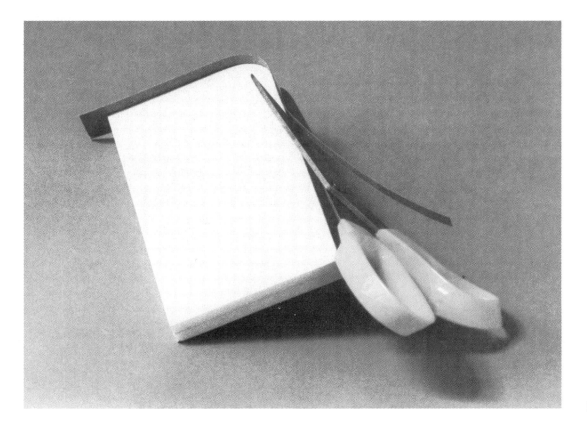

1-36. Trimming off excess paper from a border.

SPHERICAL FORMS

One of the major limitations of paper in model-building is that it cannot be used to create spherical forms. There are, however, three options available to partially overcome this problem.

The first applies to small radiuses (⅛–¼ inch/3–6mm) where it is necessary to make only one-quarter of a dome. It can be used to make concave or convex curves. The procedure involves overlapping curves, for example, in the bullnosed edge of a table corner shown in Figure 1-37.

Curve the edges of the paper as described for narrow radiuses. At the point where the axes of the curves of each edge meet, slice the paper three or four times, as though you were cutting fringe. The cuts should be as long as the curve is wide. Overlap the ends of the fringe and glue them in place. This will make the paper bow out in imitation of a sphere (Fig. 1-38).

This works best with dark one- or two-ply paper because the slices are less visible. It is not effective for large spherical forms, as the resulting shape resembles a polyhedron rather than a sphere.

The second option is to build the spherical form out of another material, such as balsa wood or high-density expanded polystyrene (Styrofoam), and then attach it to the paper model. (See Chapters 2 and 3 for information on how to build spherical inserts.) This option provides a true spherical shape but creates other problems related to visually connecting the insert to the paper model. The seam between the insert and the paper model must be covered or in some way disguised, and an effort must be made to match the colors of insert and paper (Fig. 1-39).

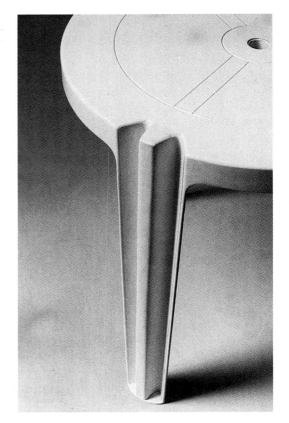

1-37. Making spherical forms with paper: a bullnosed table corner, a small-radius quarter dome made with two-ply paper.

1-38 (far left). The fringe option for making small spherical forms.

1-39. Balsa wood spherical forms painted to match the color of the paper model.

It is impossible to paint the insert in the exact color as the paper. Rather, we suggest either painting the insert in a color as similar as possible or redesigning the model so that the color difference looks intentional. Trying to match colors is acceptable when the model is white, black, or gray since slight color differences will hardly be noticeable.

In general, painting both insert and paper to match is not recommended because anything more than a very light coat of paint will make the paper warp and become hairy.

If you want to try painting the paper, use spray paint in a color close to that of the paper. Spray lightly, allow to dry, sand the paper surface with 400-grit abrasive paper; then spray another light coat of paint, allow to dry, and if the paper looks hairy, sand it again, finishing with another light coat of paint.

Matte colors should be used to minimize reflection of surface imperfections. If the desired color is not available in matte finish, spray a final coat of clear matte over the last thoroughly dry coat of color.

The third option for solving the spherical problem is not to make the spherical shape. This choice is quite consistent with the use of paper. When the problem lies in making an edge that combines two curves of different sizes lying on two different axes, it is impossible to successfully make both curves out of paper. We suggest deciding which curve will better represent the design and building only that one (Figs. 1-40, 1-41).

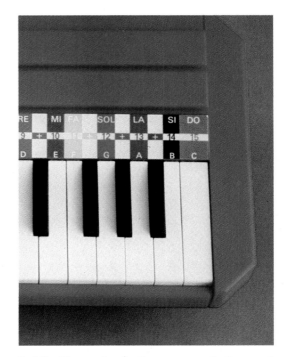

1-40. The spherical corners of the real product made out of injection-molded polystyrene.

LAMINATION

Lamination is an excellent way to strengthen a large surface. Laminating many layers of paper (four to five layers is the reasonable maximum) creates a strong structure that has a finished look. It is also possible to sandwich foamcore or chipboard between two pieces of paper to create structural pieces with a finished look.

White glue or spray adhesive may be used for laminating, although spray adhesive has distinct limitations. It is unsuitable for curved surfaces and even on flat surfaces will oxidize, causing the layers to peel away after a year or so. For a lasting bond, apply many small dots of white glue, spreading them evenly and closely to the edges.

Always glue the sheets together so that the top and bottom layers are of the same material, otherwise the lamination will warp. For example: Use one-ply paper for the first layer, chipboard for the second layer, and one-ply paper again for the third layer. Reversing the direction of the grain for each layer strengthens the lamination and further reduces the risk of warping.

It is difficult to glue together precut layers with precision. Use paper larger than needed and cut it to size when the glue has dried.

Whichever adhesive is used, it is necessary to weigh down the glued area as it dries. Heavy books are good for this purpose. Drying time varies with the number of layers glued; a rule of thumb with white glue is one hour per layer.

Lamination is an exciting technique when constructing curved surfaces; from a two-dimensional and weak material, three-dimensional and structural forms can be

1-41. The "spherical" corners of the paper model.

constructed. Lamination gives paper structural qualities similar to plywood and gives the model an outstanding strength that goes beyond all expectations.

Curving laminated paper requires a mold, either made specifically for that purpose or an improvised found object, such as a jar bottle of the desired form and radius (Fig. 1-42).

Simple curves—Preshape the paper before gluing the layers together, using the method described for preshaping wide radiuses. Glue the layers together and immediately wrap them around the mold.

To hold the lamination on the mold, wrap a protective piece of heavy paper over the lamination, then affix rubber bands around the whole assemblage. Space the rubber bands evenly around the form to avoid applying pressure to only one or two spots. Let the form dry for as many hours as there are layers of paper (Fig. 1-43).

Compound curves— More complex shapes may require that male and female molds be made. The two parts of the mold are then clamped together with C-clamps. Any combination of materials can be used to achieve the desired form, including plywood, cardboard, foamcore, and in some cases even found objects (Figs. 1-44, 1-45).

The procedure is roughly the same: Glue together oversize pieces of paper, then fit them into the mold and attach the whole assemblage with C-clamps. After the piece has fully dried, trim it to size with a knife on a cutting mat. Whenever possible, use a ruler as a guide.

Trimming small or compound curves—Sometimes a form is either too small or too complex to comfortably cut with a knife. In such cases the laminating process has to be slightly modified.

Cut out the first layer of the lamination to its finished size and preshape it. Then cut out the second layer slightly larger than the first and wrap it around the first layer, but do not glue them together. While holding the second layer around the first, mark

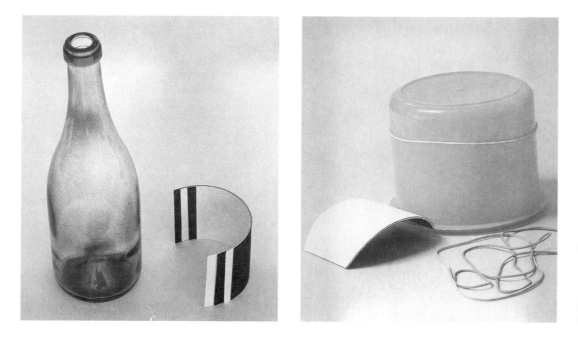

1-42 *(far left)*. **Using a bottle as a mold for a curved laminated form.**

1-43. Plastic jar mold, rubber bands, and the curved laminated piece after glue has dried.

on the inside of the second layer its desired dimension, trim it to size, and glue it to the outside of the first layer. Place the two layers in the mold, cover with protective paper, and hold in place with rubber bands or, if the curve is a complex one, with a female mold and C-clamps. Leave it to dry for one hour. Continue in this manner for all the remaining layers, waiting one hour between each layer.

This is a time-consuming process, but it results in an exceptionally sturdy structural form that is well worth the time and effort. Remember, the initial material was only

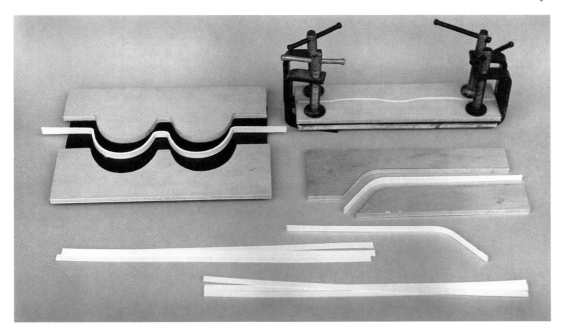

1-44. Plywood male and female molds for laminating eyeglass frames.

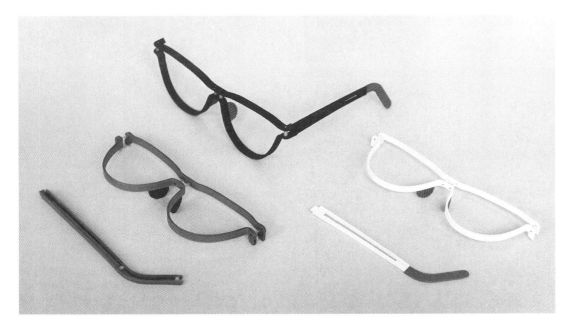

1-45. The finished laminated curved elements for eyeglass frames.

paper! The drying time can be employed building other parts of the model.

It is important to be very accurate when lining up the layers to be glued together and to be careful while placing the form around the mold. It is particularly important not to use too much glue, as the excess will ooze out between the layers when they are wrapped around or placed in the mold. Since no additional paper will be cut away, any stains will be visible on the finished lamination.

When the laminated form is dry, you may use 400-grit abrasive paper to sand away any glue drops and imperfections along the edges. As with other procedures described in this chapter, limit sanding and handling of the model so as to preserve the model's freshness.

WORKING WITH FOAMCORE AND CORRUGATED BOARD

As has been mentioned, foamcore and corrugated board are perfectly suited for use as structural supports. They can, however, also be used as the outer covering of a model, or can be laminated between multiple sheets of paper. Although many of the principles for working with paper apply also to foamcore and corrugated board, some aspects of gluing, bending, and finishing differ.

BENDING AND CURVING

Foamcore can be bent to form radiuses of various sizes. The smallest possible radius corresponds to the thickness of the foamcore being used. Use a knitting needle for bending such a narrow curve.

Do not use scoring to make curves with larger radiuses (by which we mean anything larger than the thickness of foamcore). Instead, on the back side of the foamcore mark the dimension of the arc corresponding to the desired radius; peel off the inside paper within the measured area, leaving the foam intact. Foamcore is strong because it is a sandwich structure. With one of the two external components of the sandwich structure eliminated, the structure becomes flexible and can be curved. Finally, bend the foamcore into shape (Fig. 1-46).

We suggest curving only single-faced corrugated paper. This material was created for wrapping fragile things and therefore curves and bends naturally. Bending double-faced corrugated board is possible, but the resulting radius will correspond to the board thickness (as with foamcore). It is only possible to make bends parallel to the corrugations.

1-46. A curve with a large radius built out of foamcore. Note that the paper covering has been peeled off the inside of the curve.

GLUING

White glue works well with both foamcore and corrugated board, although the porous face of corrugated board will wrinkle and become deformed if too much of this water-based adhesive is used. Solvent cements (balsa cement, rubber cement, and spray adhesive) can be used with corrugated board but may melt foamcore. Glue guns are useful when saving time and obtaining a strong bond are more important than a clean and precise job. They are unsuitable for gluing large areas, however, because the glue will dry before it is possible to spread it over the entire surface to be bonded.

To strengthen a foamcore joint made with white glue, a few straight pins evenly spaced can be pushed into the center foam. The heads of the pins can be cut off with a pair of diagonal pliers. Take care to stick them straight into the center of the core so they do not pierce the paper cover (Fig. 1-47).

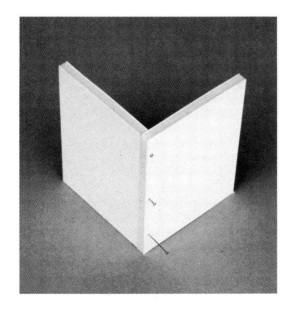

1-47. Strengthening a foamcore joint with straight pins.

FINISHING

Foamcore is by its nature a finished material, although it can be laminated with additional paper to obtain a particular color or textured surface as well as to enhance its structural qualities. Corrugated board is not a finished material and so must either be sheathed with paper or painted.

Corrugated paper can only be sheathed with three- and four-ply paper; thinner paper will show the corrugations. Use the small dots gluing technique and white glue, or spray adhesive. Avoid using too much white glue or the board will warp. Remember to sheathe both sides with exactly the same paper; different papers will warp the board.

Do not expect a good finish by painting corrugated board. Paint it only if the color is important, but remember that the quality of the surface will be poor.

The best paint for corrugated board is a matte spray paint applied in several thin layers with ample drying time between. A glossy paint will be absorbed unevenly, yielding a surface that is shiny in places and matte in others. Water-based paints are usually matte, but they must be used in very thin coats to avoid wrinkling the paper face.

SPECIAL EFFECTS

Final touches are what complete the look of the model and increase its realism. It is possible to represent metal or plastic surfaces that are shiny or textured, grooves and beads on sheet metal, plastic moldings and dyecasts, grilles, and indentations.

ADHESIVE FOILS

Adhesive-backed foils can be used effectively to give the appearance of metal or plastic with either a shiny or textured finish (Fig. 1-48).

Avoid covering an area larger than 12 by 12 inches (300 × 300mm) with adhesive foil, since it is difficult to apply it with precision and to avoid having air bubbles between the model surface and the adhesive foil. In addition, large expanses of adhesive foil look cheap since foils are made from very thin inexpensive plastic.

An alternative when a large area is to be covered is colored or metallic paper. (See Fig. 1-51 for an example of metallic paper.)

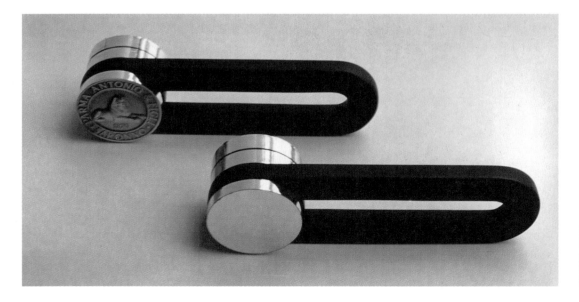

1-48. Two 1:1 scale models of safe door handles. The cylindrical parts are two-ply paper covered with chrome finish adhesive foil. The handles were cut out from ³/₈-inch (10mm) balsa sheet and painted black.

Avoid "wood-look" adhesive foils. More credible and elegant treatments include a sheet of balsa (Fig. 1-49) or veneer for small areas (see Chapter 3) or Canson Mi-Teintes paper for large areas. This paper has a warm feeling and texture similar to wood but a more abstract look. Always consider the look of the design, not just the model-making technique, and weigh realism against other factors.

Before applying adhesive foil to the surface of the model, be sure to remove any cutting debris, dust, hair, and excess glue, as these will show up as bumps under the foil. Cut out a piece of foil larger than the area to be covered, leaving on the backing. Slowly peel off a part of the backing; begin rolling the foil onto the model while rubbing it to push out any air bubbles. Press hard with your fingertips, a tissue, or a soft rag to smooth out any wrinkles or bubbles; never use a sharp tool, which will scratch and mark the foil. If a few air bubbles do form, pierce them with a compass point and press to expel the air.

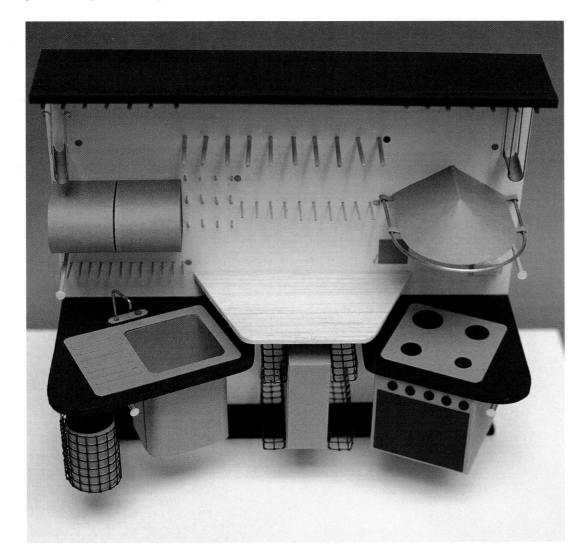

1-49. Scale model (1:10) of a kitchen unit (designed by the authors). The kitchen counter is made of balsa wood. The sink top, range top, top shelf, and back panel are foamcore covered with two- and three-ply paper. The baskets are metal-welded mesh. The range hood bar was made with $^1/_{16}$-inch (1.5mm) piano wire; yellow paper dots and $^1/_{32}$-inch (0.8mm) piano wire were used for other details.

Applying adhesive foil to a curved surface may seem easy since the foil comes in a roll; however, it is the backing paper, not the foil, that is curved. When covering a curve always tape down the foil at the least visible end of the curve to stop it from peeling back with time. Use clear polyester tape on glossy foils and matte-finish acetate tape on matte foils. Taping is necessary only for curved surfaces with a radius of ⅝ inch (15mm) or less.

GROOVES AND BEADS

Grooves can be made by using two layers of paper of the same color. One layer is used for cutting out the groove and the other layer is for reproducing the same color under the groove; the effect is of a solid piece, not two layers (Fig. 1-50).

With a pencil lightly mark the dimensions of the groove on one of the sheets. Cut out the ends of the groove with a hollow punch, then connect the two round holes by cutting the straight sections with a knife (see Making Oval, Square, Rectangular, Triangular Holes in this chapter). Finally, glue the two pieces of paper together using the same process as described in the beginning of the section on lamination. Be careful not to spread the glue too closely to the groove.

Narrow grooves of ¹⁄₃₂ to ¹⁄₁₆ inch (0.8–1.5mm) also can be represented with strips of black adhesive foil or charting tape cut to size. Be sure to press the tape or foil down very hard; since there is such a small adhesive area in contact with the model's surface it may otherwise peel off in time (Fig. 1-51).

1-50. Scale model (1:3) of an air-conditioning unit (designed by the authors). Note the groove on the front panel and the use of black paper to suggest grille openings. See also Figure 1-64.

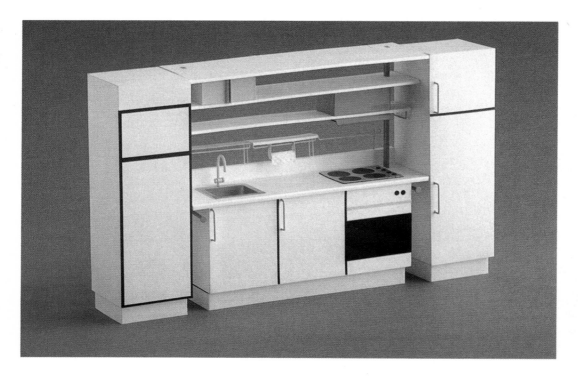

1-51. Strips of black adhesive foil used to represent grooves on cabinets and refrigerator in the scale model (1:10) of a kitchen unit (designed by the authors). Metallic finish paper is used for the sink; door handles and other details are made out of piano wire. See also Figure 14-16.

Beads are somehow the negative of grooves and are therefore made like grooves. Use white glue, rubber cement, or spray adhesive depending on how long the model should last.

Beads are easier and faster to make than grooves. Using the same color paper as the surface of the model, cut out narrow strips or any other shape (lettering, decorations). Follow the instructions given in the beginning of this section. Avoid using an excessive amount of glue and be sure to weigh down the strips with books while the glue is drying (Figs. 1-52, 1-53, 1-54).

1-52. Beads and relief lettering on a 1:1 scale model of a bathroom scale with a vinyl mat (designed by the authors). Yellow three-ply paper was coated with yellow paint to soften the edges.

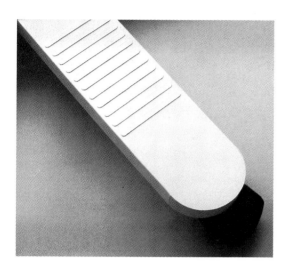

1-53. Detail, model of a star-base for office chair showing the textured surface of one branch of the star.

1-54. Detail, textured surface of a folding chair's seat (1:1 scale). Texture was achieved by gluing together two layers of black three-ply paper. The outer layer consists of parallel strips of paper separated by grooves.

SHALLOW DRAWING

We have already given an example of shallow drawing in the section on Round Holes (see Fig. 1-18); various other shapes usually obtained by shallow drawing on sheet metal can be imitated with paper. One of the most effective uses is for a rim around an opening (Fig. 1-55). Two- or three-ply paper should be used for the part of the model that has the shallow drawn detail.

A specially made die is needed to reproduce the shallow drawing effect. Use a jigsaw to cut an opening in a piece of ¼-inch (6mm) plywood (see Tools, Chapter 3). This opening in the piece of plywood will perform the function of a female mold to produce a shallow drawn rim in the paper. Use a file and then 60-grit abrasive paper to round the edge of the rim. The radius of the die should not exceed ⅛ inch (3mm).

Leave some extra paper on the interior of the opening (cut a smaller hole than necessary); it will be needed for the shallow drawn rim (Fig. 1-56). Gently rub a stick of hardwood over the portion of paper that juts inside the opening of the plywood board. Do not rub so hard that you tear the paper or spoil its surface (Figs. 1-57, 1-58).

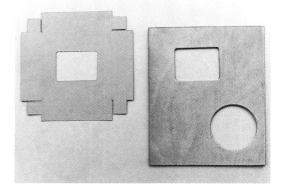

1-56. Shallow drawing: precut paper (left) and plywood die (right).

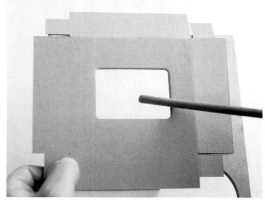

1-57. Shallow drawing: rubbing paper with a wooden stick to create a shallow-drawn effect.

1-55. Shallow drawn rims around the openings of a gas heater's control panel.

1-58. Shallow drawn paper rims.

TEXTURES

Photoengraved textures on plastic surfaces can be imitated with adhesive foils, if the right color is available. Otherwise, abrasive paper spraypainted with the appropriate color can be used. Use matte paint, or if unavailable, use glossy paint, and follow with a coat of clear matte finish (Fig. 1-59).

A simpler option, a self-adhesive tone (Letratone), produces a two-dimensional imitation of the photoengraved texture.

Parallel lines, if not too deep, can be made by gluing strips of paper of the appropriate color to the surface, as described for grooves and beads. If the lines should have round profiles, use single-faced corrugated paper spraypainted with the appropriate matte color (Fig. 1-60).

Small circles cut out with a hollow punch can be used to imitate buttons or an embossed texture. Lightly mark their position on the model, then apply small dots of white glue and position circles with tweezers. If there are many circles to apply, a lot of patience is required when positioning them so that the job does not look haphazard (Fig. 1-61).

Grilles on loudspeakers, air intakes, and exhaust grilles can be easily and quickly represented with accordion-folded paper. For large grilles, the openings can be shown by attaching black strips of paper or matte black adhesive foil to the inner angle of each fold (Figs. 1-62, 1-63, 1-64).

1-59. Imitation of photoengraved texture on the 1:4 scale model of a plastic chair.

1-60. Model (1:1 scale) of an office chair (designed by the authors). Single-faced corrugated paper, painted to match the color of the model, renders a plastic textured surface.

1-61. Textured dot finish made by gluing punched out circles of three-ply paper to model surface.

1-62 *(below).* Model (1:1 scale) of a portable air-conditioning unit (designed by the authors), showing the textured handle and grille. The grille effect was achieved using accordion-folded three-ply paper.

1-63. The speaker grille on a 1:1 scale model of a television set (designed by the authors). As in Figure 1-62, accordion-folded three-ply paper was used.

To depict round, rectangular, and square LEDs (light-emitting diodes) use black paper to surround a brightly colored paper which represents the light.

The black paper under the colored dot adds depth, giving a three-dimensional effect. Do not be tempted to use black ink instead of paper; a painted dot will look cheap and it will not give a three-dimensional effect.

If the LED is round, use a hollow punch to cut out the paper dot. For other shapes use a knife or curved nail scissors. Cut out the colored paper to the desired size of the LED, then cut out the black paper in the same shape but slightly larger.

Apply a small dot of white glue to the center of the black paper and position the colored paper dot precisely with tweezers (Fig. 1-65).

Many more special effects can be created with paper and the other materials described in this chapter. The demands of the design and the imagination of the designer, combined with the experience acquired working with paper, will lead to creative solutions.

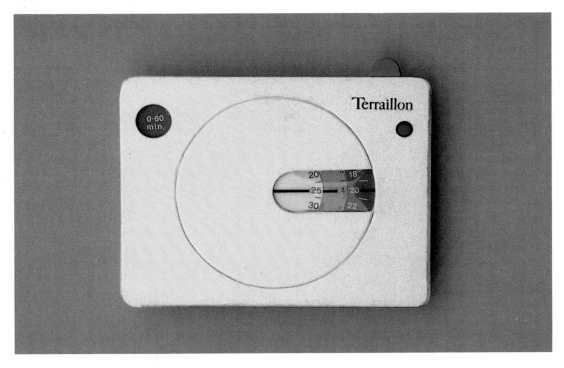

1-65. Two-dimensional model of an electronic timer (designed by the authors). Red LED in the upper right corner.

1-64 (facing page, bottom right). The air exhaust on the model of the portable air-conditioning unit seen in Figure 1-62. Black paper was used to represent the openings. See also Figure 1-50.

Expanded resins, or foams, are plastic materials into which air or a gas has been introduced during the polymerization process to reduce their density. Originally developed as insulating and packaging materials, foams are now widely used for model-making because they are soft, easy to work with, and require very little workshop equipment.

Expanded resins can be divided between rigid and soft foams. We rarely use soft foams except for representing the look of upholstery. We use rigid foams quite often for various types of models.

Expanded resins are not as easy to find as paper. Because they are strictly speaking insulating and packaging materials, sources for them include lumberyards and home improvement centers as well as model and art supply stores. Listings in the Yellow Pages under the headings *plastic, foam and sponge rubber,* and *packaging materials* as well as the names of specific resins may include dealers specializing in these products.

The advantage expanded resins have over most other model-making materials is that models can be built from them very quickly. Their aesthetic qualities, however, leave much to be desired. All expanded resins, with the exception of polymethacrylimid, are porous, so the surface finish is poor. In line with our quick and easy approach we recommend that expanded resins be used, as much as possible, as they are, without undergoing heavy finishing. The time and effort spent on trying to improve the look of a foam surface (by repeatedly filling, sanding, and painting) will result instead in destruction of the precision and freshness of the model. The designer who wishes to invest such a huge amount of time will get better results with harder materials, such as wood or polyester reinforced with glass fibers (Fiberglas), or more sophisticated techniques, such as vacuum forming.

MATERIALS

RIGID FOAMS

Expanded polystyrene (Styrofoam)—one of the least expensive and easiest to find; suitable only for rough models. Use only high-density foam (minimum 1.9 pounds per cubic foot/30kg per m³); anything less dense will crumble easily. Even high-density foam is porous and fragile, but it is fast and easy to model. Its elastic qualities may cause it to lose its shape during the building process (Fig. 2-1).

Extruded polystyrene—more compact and homogeneous than expanded polystyrene; has a more refined surface and is structurally stronger. Extruded polystyrene was developed as a waterproof thermoinsulating material. Most shops will stock only expanded polystyrene, which has similar thermal properties but, because it is not waterproof, is cheaper (Fig. 2-2).

Polyurethane—a thermosetting resin chemically quite different from the polystyrenes. Better suited for precision work, it is more brittle, less elastic, and therefore less likely to lose its shape. Use only high-density material (approximately 2.5 pounds per cubic foot/40kg per m³). Produces an irritating dust so a protective mask should be worn when working with this material. The porous surface yields a nice matte finish when painted (Fig. 2-3).

Polymethacrylimid (Rohacell)—by far the best and most expensive of the expanded resins; conceived specifically for model-making and for structural applications in the aircraft industry. Strong, compact, and homogeneous, it has a fairly smooth surface and is easy and pleasant to work with. Resembles extruded polystyrene in appearance but is far superior in its working qualities. Its high cost can be prohibitive, and for large models it may be better to use extruded polystyrene; this would leave the designer free to discard a model and start over if the first one did not come out well. May be difficult to find (Fig. 2-4).

2-1. Expanded polystyrene.

2-2 (above). Extruded polystyrene.

2-3 (far left). Rigid polyurethane foam.

2-4. Polymethacrylimid foam (Rohacell).

SOFT FOAMS

Polyurethane—of limited use for scale models because it is difficult to find in thicknesses under ⅜ inch (10mm); even in high-density forms too soft for precision work. Recommended for 1:1 scale models of upholstery (Fig. 2-5).

Foam rubber—easy to work with; comes in high densities and narrow thicknesses, usually available in black only. Ideal for upholstery on scale models of chairs and other furniture; excellent for imitating self-skinning polyurethane upholstery (Fig. 2-6).

Polyethylene—easy to work with; often available in high densities, narrow thicknesses, and several colors. This last possibility, combined with its texture, recommends its use in imitating fabric-upholstered furniture (Fig. 2-7).

2-5. Soft polyurethane foam.

2-6. Foam rubber.

2-7. Expanded polyethylene.

Tools

Tools for working with expanded resins fall into two categories: cutting tools and finishing tools.

CUTTING TOOLS

Cutting tools should be used only to cut the rough shape or the outline of the form out of the foam block or sheet. Different cutting tools are appropriate for each of the expanded resins.

Hot-wire cutters—for polystyrene and polymethacrylimid up to ½ inch (12mm) thick; particularly good for expanded and extruded polystyrene. Heat produced by the flow of electrical current through the wire locally melts the expanded resin. The temperature of the wire must be accurately regulated according to the type and density of the resin being cut. If the wire is too hot the cut will be too wide and uneven; if the wire is too cold the pressure applied during cutting will deform the wire and may break it. Always make a sample cut on a piece of scrap foam first. Hot-wire cutters are for cutting and carving rough shapes only, not for producing a finished surface.

Available at hobby and art supply stores, good hot-wire cutters are very expensive. Two simple but efficient hot-wire cutters can be made following the steps illustrated in Figures 2-8, 2-9, and 2-10. Be sure to use electrical parts that conform to local code.

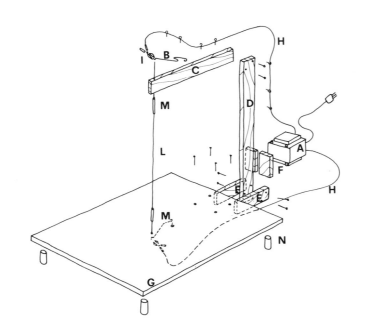

2-8. Assembly drawing of a general-purpose hot-wire cutter. See Figure 2-10 top for photo of finished device.

A. Transformer 100 W outlet 12 V
B. Piano wire spring (⁵⁄₆₄ inch/2mm) for keeping hot wire in tension
C. 1 by 2 by 16-inch (25 × 50 × 400mm) pine strip
D. 1 by 2 by 20-inch (25 × 50 × 500mm) pine strip
E. 1 by 2 by 8-inch (25 × 50 × 200mm) pine strip
F. 1 by 2 by 6-inch (25 × 50 × 150mm) pine strip
G. 1 by 20 by 30-inch (25 × 500 × 750mm) laminated plastic board (Formica)
H. Insulated electrical wire
I. Two alligator clips
L. Nickel-chromium wire ¹⁄₆₄ inch (0.4mm) thick, 20 inch (500mm) long
M. 2 brass or aluminum tubes for shielding wood from heat
N. 4 feet

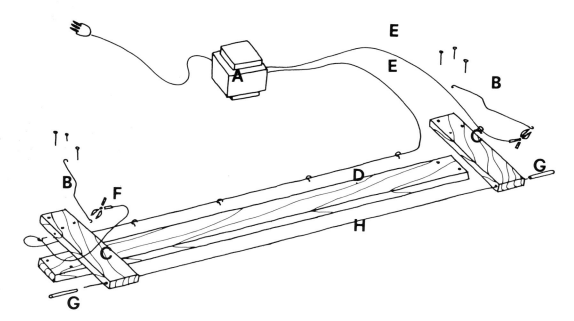

2-9. Assembly drawing of hot-wire cutter used for cutting cylindrical and similar shapes with a low base-to-height ratio. See Figure 2-10 bottom for photo of finished device.

A. Transformer 100 W outlet 24 V
B. Piano wire spring (⁵⁄₆₄ inch/2mm) for keeping hot wire in tension
C. 1 by 2 by 8-inch (25 × 50 × 200mm) pine strip
D. 1 by 2 by 28-inch (25 × 50 × 700mm) pine strip
E. Insulated electrical wire
F. Two alligator clips
G. Two brass or aluminum tubes for shielding wood from heat
H. Nickel-chromium wire ¹⁄₆₄ inch (0.4mm) thick, 30 inch (750mm) long

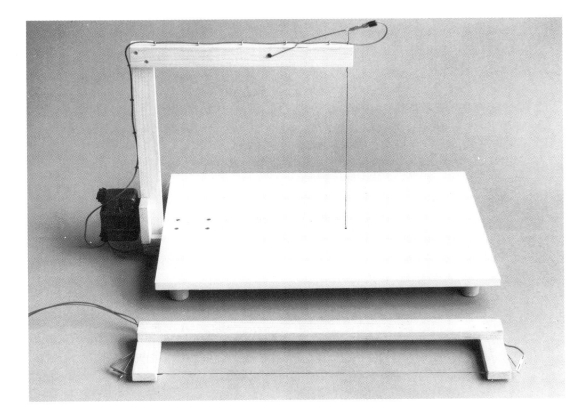

2-10. Hot-wire cutters: general-purpose (top) and for cylindrical shapes (bottom).

Handsaw—for polyurethane and for polymethacrylimid thicker than ½ inch (12mm). Select a saw with a thin blade and closely spaced teeth. If it has a steel backing along the top of the blade, remove it to make it easier to cut through thick pieces. Never use on polystyrene foam; it is a low-resiliency material that will turn to dust along the cutting edge (Fig. 2-11).

Hacksaw blade—excellent for cutting most rigid expanded resins (including high-density extruded polystyrene). Since most foams are quite easy to cut, the blade can be used without a handle, making this blade particularly good for contouring shapes.

Knives—a mat knife with a replaceable, nonretractable blade, such as the Stanley recommended for use with paper, for cutting rigid foams up to ⅜ inch (10mm) thick and all soft expanded resins with similar thicknesses. Recommended for rough non-precision work. Snap-off knives, such as those described in Chapter 1, can be used on soft foams but are inadequate for cutting hard foams.

Scissors—for cutting all types of soft foams and for rounding their edges. Choose straight-bladed scissors with asymmetrical handles, such as Fiskars.

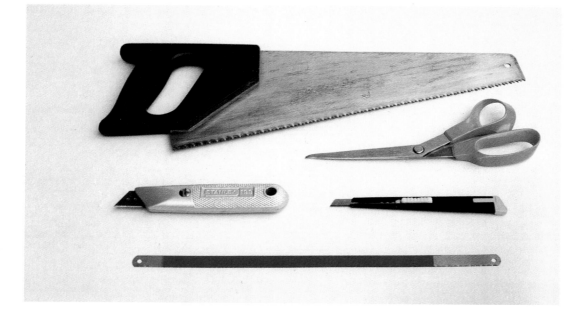

2-11. Cutting tools (top to bottom): hand-saw, scissors, utility knives, hacksaw blade.

SANDING AND FINISHING TOOLS

Sanding blocks and pads are the basic tools for working on rigid foams. After the rough shape is cut, all other operations, like rounding corners and edges and making grooves and other sculptured details on the surface of the model, must be done with a sanding block of the appropriate shape to which abrasive paper is attached with double-coated adhesive tape or contact cement.

Once a part of the surface has been treated with abrasive paper, the rest must be finished using abrasive paper as well. For hard materials and rough shaping, use 80- to 100-grit; finer grades (200- to 400-grit) are suited for the finishing job and for making the surface of the whole model uniform. Attach the paper very carefully to the sanding pad or block; any wrinkles will spoil the foam's surface during sanding.

Plywood board—minimum size: 12 by 12 by ¾ inch (300 × 300 × 20mm); for finishing large areas of the model and for obtaining true, smooth, plane surfaces.

Plywood pads—Three sizes are needed: small (1 by 3 inches/25 × 75mm), medium (2 by 4 inches/50 × 100mm), and large (2 by 8 inches/50 × 200mm). The small one is for sanding narrow radiuses and small flat areas that the other blocks are too big for. The medium and large ones are for making cylinders and other rounded shapes, and for finishing small flat surfaces (Fig. 2-12).

Cylinders and cones—various diameters; they can be wooden dowels, glass or hard plastic bottles, metal tubes, or tubes expressly made of four-ply paper. Cylinders are used for holes and other concave cylindrical shapes; cones are primarily used for enlarging holes (Fig. 2-13).

Concave pads—make them out of wood, foamcore, or cardboard with specific radiuses; used to form convex circular shapes (Fig. 2-14).

2-12. Sanding tools: plywood board and large, medium, and small plywood pads.

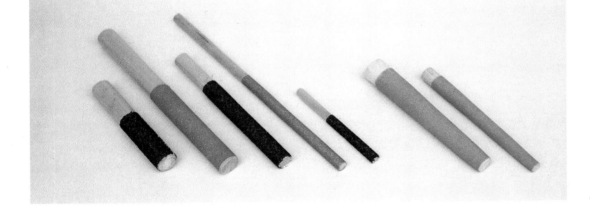

2-13. Sanding tools: small cylinders and cones.

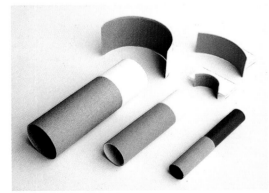

2-14. Sanding tools: concave pads and cylinders.

Special shapes—designed and built of foamcore, cardboard, balsa wood, or found objects to suit a specific shape. Once they are built they will last for a long time and thus they become part of your permanent equipment (Fig. 2-15).

STRAIGHTEDGES

Ruler—choose a heavyweight metal one, not wood or plastic.

Square—use carpenter's squares or try squares made of metal rather than wood or plastic because they are heavy and very durable (Fig. 2-16).

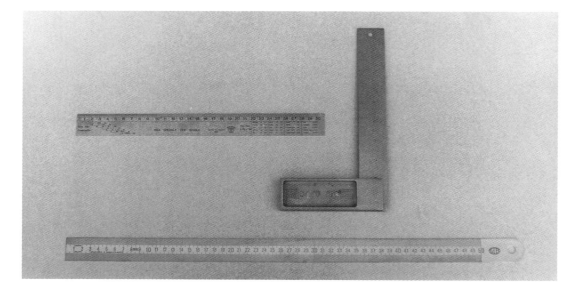

2-15. Sanding tools: A sanding stick made especially for carving out U-shaped grooves.

2-16. Metal rulers and a try square.

ADHESIVES

Contact cement—all-purpose glue for nearly all foams, both rigid and soft, available under various trade names. Polystyrene foam requires a formulation made specifically for it since other contact cements will melt the foam. (Look for the words *polystyrene foam* on the label, not just *polystyrene*.)

Spray adhesive—related to contact cement but suitable for all foams, including polystyrene foam.

Epoxy—can be used on both rigid and soft expanded resins. Because the joint will be harder than the joint made with contact cement and also harder than the foam itself, it is particularly important not to spread the glue close to the edge.

White glue—suitable only for low-density expanded polystyrene under 1 inch (25mm) thick. Because it is a water-based glue, it needs air to dry; anything thicker than 1 inch will not admit sufficient air and will, therefore, take a very long time to dry.

Tesa Coll—very good glue for polystyrene foam. Although it is actually a multipurpose glue, it can be employed on polystyrene foam. It must be used like contact cement: Spread the glue on both surfaces to be glued and let dry before joining the surfaces together (Fig. 2-17).

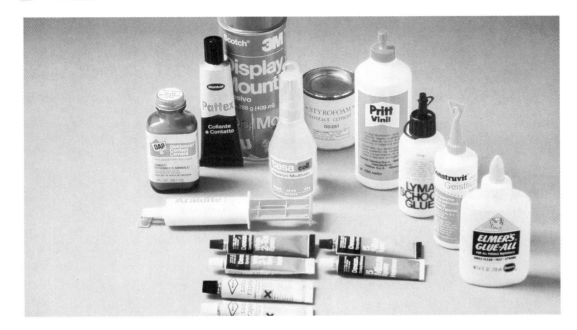

2-17. An international selection of adhesives for expanded resins: contact cements (left); glues for polystyrene foam—spray adhesive, Tesa Coll, Styrofoam contact cement (top center); white glues (right); epoxy glues (center and bottom).

WORKING WITH EXPANDED RESINS

Unlike paper, with which it is possible to design without a preliminary drawing since the structure of the material is always present as a guide for the construction of the shape, foams require a clear plan or drawing. Foams are homogeneous and are similar to amorphous materials. Without a clear plan, there is the risk of sanding away the whole block of expanded resin without obtaining the form you had in mind.

We suggest drawing the three views of the model on a sheet of four-ply or, better, a piece of cardboard. Then cut out the three views and use them as templates for both tracing onto the foam and cutting out the form.

TRACING

The first step is to cut a foam block from a bigger block of expanded resin (with a saw or hot-wire cutter) to create a geometric prism that has the overall dimensions of

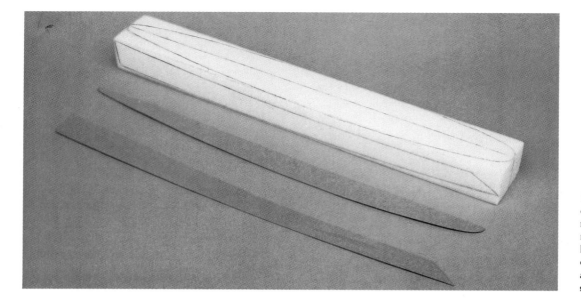

2-18. Tracing two of the three views of a catamaran hull (1:20 scale) onto a block of rigid polyurethane foam. The third view was not traced onto the foam because it would have had to represent too many different cross sections. On small models, two views are usually enough to obtain the desired shape.

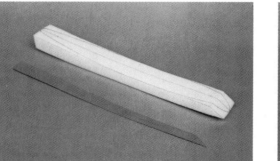

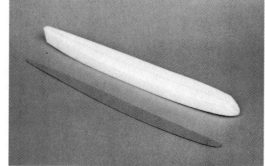

2-19, 2-20. The hull's shape is cut out following the traced views.

2-21. The hull's final shape, refined with sanding pads.

the model. Next, draw two or three views of the model, and then trace them with pencil onto the block of expanded resin (Fig. 2-18). Finally, cut out the form with a hot wire or a saw (Figs. 2-19, 2-20, 2-21).

CUTTING

Never work freehand with rigid expanded resins. Being low-density material, they are quite yielding and it is easy for an unguided hand to cut off or to sand away too much.

Using a hot wire—It is a good idea to practice on scrap foam before doing a final cut. Pressure, speed, and temperature are all significant variables in achieving a neat cut. Too much force on the wire and too much pressure against the template will result in a nonorthogonal cut. The cutting speed is directly proportional to the wire temperature. If the speed is too low and the temperature is high, the cut will be too wide and uneven. Maintain a constant cutting speed and never stop at any point along the cut, otherwise the material around the wire will melt, creating a hole.

Using a saw blade—The challenge when cutting foam blocks, which are generally thick, is keeping the cut orthogonal. We suggest tracing the form to be cut onto both sides of the block or applying a template to each of the opposite sides of the block.

Avoid circular cuts. The saw blade is flat and will never follow the pattern exactly. Instead, make a series of straight cuts to create a sort of polygonal shape, then round with sanding pads of the right size and shape (Figs. 2-22, 2-23).

When cutting soft expanded resins with a knife, be sure to apply a lot of pressure to the ruler so as to prevent the blade from pulling and tearing the foam. We suggest cutting soft foams with scissors, after having traced the form to be cut with a felt tip pen, possibly with the help of a paper or cardboard template.

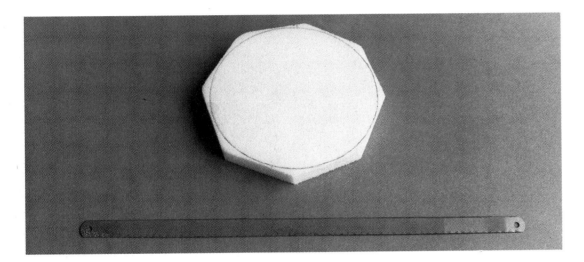

2-22. Cutting out a circular shape from rigid polyurethane foam with a saw blade. Note the polygonal shape.

2-23. The true circular shape is obtained with a concave sanding pad.

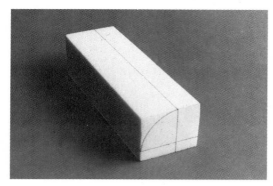

2-24. Building a round profile: Tracing.

2-25, 2-26. Building a round profile: Excess foam trimmed off.

SHAPING

Expanded resins are better suited for models with nongeometric shapes. Cutting and sanding can be done by feel, working as a sculptor does with the flowing smoothness of the shape. Nonetheless, we offer some tips on making round profiles and plane surfaces.

Round profiles—present a particular problem, especially for beginners: how to obtain a constant radius. Working with templates helps.

First trace the two round forms corresponding to the section of the profile onto both extremities of the foam block (Fig. 2-24), or use double-coated tape to stick two templates onto the opposite ends of the block. Trace a tangent to the round form, again on both extremities. Trim off the foam by following the tangent line (Fig. 2-25). Trace two more tangent lines onto the area of the curve where no cut has been made (again on both sides). Trim off the extra foam by following the tangent lines (Fig. 2-26). Now round the edges with sanding pads (Fig. 2-27). Frequently check the shape against the light using a counter or negative template (Fig. 2-28). The surface can be evened out with 300- or 400-grit abrasive paper.

Plane surfaces—always hard to obtain. The beginner tends to place inconsistent pressure on the sanding block while passing it over the surface of the model, and a convex surface results. To ensure a true plane surface, follow these three rules:

1. Use the largest possible sanding pad or a large sanding board.
2. While sanding, place more pressure on the pad as you pass it over the center of the surface and less near the edges.
3. Frequently test the flatness of the surface with a ruler or try square.

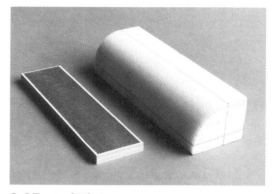

2-27. Building a round profile: Edges rounded with a sanding pad.

2-28. Building a round profile: Checking the shape with a paper template.

GLUING

The most important thing to remember when gluing foam is never to spread any type of glue close to the edge. The distance from the edge should be proportionate to the size of the pieces being glued together. If the glue is placed too close to the edge, there will be a ridge between the two pieces when the surface is sanded, due to the fact that the glue is harder than the foam and resistant to abrasive paper. For the same reason, do not put any glue on visible surfaces or on surfaces that will be sanded.

PAINTING

We do not recommend using filler on expanded resins. Filling one or two spots will show up more than the original gaps; the very porous foam surface will therefore contrast greatly with the patched area. Filling the entire surface of the model is an endless job that leads to poor results.

It is best simply to paint the model, taking advantage of the textured look of the porous surface. All paints should be sprayed on.

Buying spray cans is simpler, cleaner, and less complicated than using an airgun and compressor. A wide range of colors and formulations, even water-based paints, are available in spray cans. Use paints packaged in non-flourocarbon spray cans whenever possible.

Always use matte colors. Water-based paints are usually available only in a matte finish, whereas solvent-based paints may not be available in all colors in matte finish. In that case, apply a final coat of clear matte paint.

Expanded polystyrene should be painted only with water-based paints because solvent paints will melt the polystyrene. Sand the entire surface to be painted with 360- or 400-grit abrasive paper; spray with one light coat of paint; sand again, but very lightly, and then spray on the final coat of paint. It is always better to cover the model with two light coats of paint instead of one heavy coat.

Polyurethane and polymethacrylimid foams can be painted with any type of paint, except for emulsion paints, which spoil polymethacrylimid. These two foams need to be sanded only once and then can be painted with as many coats as required. Apply very light coats, because heavy painting will unevenly fill the surface's pores.

If two or more parts need to be painted with different colors, do not mask the model with adhesive tape. Instead, spraypaint the parts separately and then assemble them.

Painting is discussed in greater detail in Chapter 3.

3  WOOD

Wood is widely used in traditional model-making. A foundry model-maker carves a shape with a chisel from a solid block of wood; a hobbyist uses strip planking to build streamlined shapes like ship hulls and airplane fuselages. Both techniques produce exciting results but require accomplished craftsmanship and a lot of time.

Although it is a very demanding material, wood can be used in simpler ways, in line with the quick and easy model-making techniques we practice. We generally use wood for detail work and as a complementary material. We rarely use it for full-scale models, which would entail having a fully equipped workshop and professional woodworking equipment as well as extra staff. And we never build models entirely out of wood, which would require, among other things, extensive finishing work. Rather we use it in combination with finished materials such as paper and plastic, a time- and energy-saving strategy.

MATERIALS

Most of the wood we use can be found in art supply and model shops. We recommend these sources because they carry the type of wood in the dimensions needed for our kinds of models. Lumberyards usually will sell only larger quantities and larger dimensions, and primarily hardwoods and plywood (Fig. 3-1).

3-1. Different types of wood (top to bottom, left to right): plywood; balsa strips and dowels; hardwood strips.

BALSA WOOD

Balsa is very soft and easy to cut. It requires neither special glues nor difficult gluing techniques. The two main drawbacks are that it is delicate and very grainy. Although it is tempting to think that one could build almost anything out of balsa, its delicacy makes it unsuitable for many structural parts, which may be better made from hardwood. The time saved in cutting and gluing balsa may be lost in the finishing stage, trying to cover its grain.

Balsa is available in a great variety of shapes and sizes. Planks, sheets, square and rectangular strips, and dowels are the most common shapes; in addition, many model shops also carry triangular, half round, and quarter round strips.

Avoid working with balsa in very thin strips or very large planks or blocks. Strips less than ⅛ by ⅛ inch (3 × 3mm) are structurally weak and break easily. Planks and blocks are available in dimensions up to 6 by 6 inches (150 × 150mm), but they are quite expensive. In addition, shaping and finishing big pieces of balsa are messy jobs that require a lot of time. For large models, expanded resins are a better choice.

HARDWOOD

Although it may seem irreverent to the long and noble tradition of woodworking to discuss all of the many different hardwoods under a single heading, the scope and purpose of this book dictate doing so. With pieces of wood as small as we use, the working characteristics of a particular hardwood matter very little. The choice of wood should be made in terms of what is available and the aesthetic look desired.

Basswood, birch, mahogany, spruce, and walnut usually come in strips and dowels. As with balsa, strips may be square or rectangular and come in many sizes; occasionally other sections (triangular, half round) are available. Since these sections generally have small dimensions, they are almost as easily cut as balsa. Hardwood grain is more compact than balsa and other soft woods, making painting an easier and faster job.

PLYWOOD

We generally use plywood as a complementary material, rather than a primary building material. Although universally available at lumberyards, plywood for model-making is better purchased at a slightly higher price in hobby shops, where it will be found in a higher quality and in dimensions suited for the task.

Plywood intended for models (in thicknesses ranging from $1/32$ to $3/16$ inch/0.7–5mm) is very compact and fine-grained, requiring less finishing work.

VENEER

A veneer is a thin layer of wood used to cover particle board, giving the effect of solid wood. Veneers of different types of wood can be bought at lumberyards. In our models, we use veneers to represent the wood surface on cabinets, tables, and other objects that are meant to be in wood.

We deal with veneer as we do with paper: cutting it with a utility knife and gluing it onto foamcore with white glue. Because white glue slightly wrinkles the veneer surface, we finish by sanding, which yields a very smooth surface and eliminates any glue stains (Fig. 3-2).

3-2. Veneer sheets.

TOOLS

KNIVES

The three basic tools for cutting balsa wood up to ¼ inch (6mm) thick are the same knives used with paper: a mat knife like the Stanley with a replaceable, nonretractable blade; a snap-off knife with a metal or metal-reinforced handle like the Olfa 180; and an X-Acto knife.

The Stanley knife, with its large, strong blade and big handle, can be used for cutting hardwood strips up to ³⁄₁₆ by ³⁄₁₆ inch (5 × 5mm) and plywood up to ⅛ inch (3mm) thick. Using a knife for straight cuts and on small wood strips is faster and more accurate than using a saw. Using a knife on thick or very hard woods, however, will take a long time to produce an imprecise cut.

SAWS

Jigsaw—for cutting curves and other complex shapes (corners, zig-zags) in thick balsa and plywood. Hand jigsaw sets with a wooden tablet that can be clamped to any tabletop are available in model shops. The tablet protects the table edge from damage and helps in cutting complex shapes. Electric jigsaws are expensive and, unless one wants to specialize in wood, are not necessary.

Jeweler's saw—an all-purpose saw for model-makers; a small hacksaw is a good substitute for cutting hardwood strips, dowels, and thick balsa sheets (Fig. 3-3).

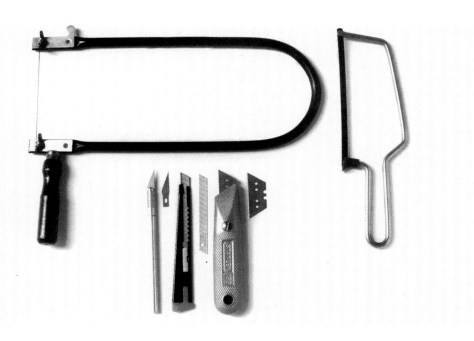

3-3. Cutting tools: jigsaw (top left); jeweler's saw (top right); utility knives and their blades—X-Acto, snap-off, mat knife (center, left to right).

DRILLS

Electric drills are so inexpensive and so handy that we recommend them over hand drills. The movement of the operator's hand as it rotates a hand drill may affect the precision of the hole being drilled. For model-making, two types of drill are needed: a regular portable drill and a miniature drill. A useful accessory for precision work is a drill press stand.

The regular drill should be used for holes over $\frac{1}{8}$ inch (3mm) in diameter. The weight of the tool makes it difficult to work with the precision necessary for smaller holes and will eventually break the thin twist drill point.

There are many miniature electric drills on the market, some of them battery operated. The best known is the Dremel, which also has a large variety of accessories. Look for a miniature drill that is lightweight and has a chuck that can take twist drill points as thin as .5mm.

FINISHING TOOLS

Files—essential tools for model-makers. Files should be of high quality; if the quality is poor, the files will merely spoil the wood, not bite into it.

A big 12-inch (300mm) half round (see Fig. 3-5) or flat medium to fine grade file is required for filing large surfaces and, most of all, for surface smoothing and squaring. This latter option spares the model-maker the need to learn how to use a plane and the bother of having to sharpen the blade.

Also essential is a set of small files: round, triangular, flat, half round, for rounding corners, modifying holes (from round to polygonal), making indentations, and for other similar jobs (Fig. 3-4).

Abrasive paper—used mostly to finish the wood surface, not, as with foams, for shaping. In general, a sanding block is not needed except when it is necessary to work on a true plane surface. In this case, the abrasive paper should be supported with the largest possible block of wood. When abrasive paper is used alone, we suggest folding a small sheet two to four times, so that it is stiff and does not take the shape of your fingertips (Fig. 3-5).

At a minimum, keep on hand the following grits: 60 for rounding corners; 100 for removing filler. Use finer grits for balsa (80 instead of 60).

WORK SURFACES

The semihard plastic mat, although excellent for cutting, is not a practical work surface for wood. A sheet of plywood (18 by 24 by $\frac{1}{2}$ inches/450 × 600 × 12mm) is handier because it can be used as a surface plate for assembling parts of the model,

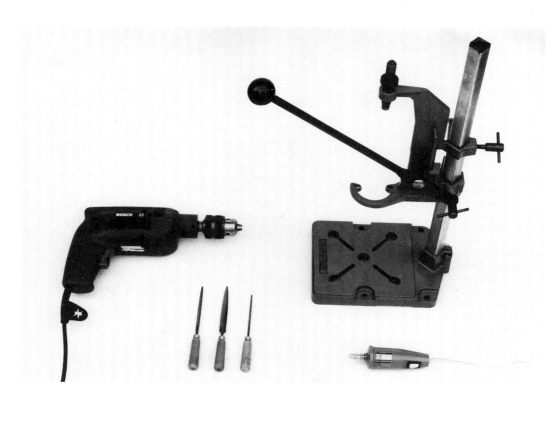

3-4. Electric drill (left); drill press stand (right); a set of small files (center); miniature drill (bottom right).

3-5. Finishing tools (left to right): A 12-inch half round file; wooden sanding blocks; abrasive paper of various grits.

for testing parts that must have flat surfaces, and for checking alignment and perpendicularity with rulers and try squares. Furthermore, small nails and pins can be stuck into its surface to hold in place pieces to be glued. Fixing a small vise to the board will convert it into a portable and storable workbench.

HOLDING AND CLAMPING TOOLS

Small vise—attached to a building board, an indispensable tool for holding in place wood strips to be cut and refined. For precision work it is always best to avoid hand holding the piece to be cut or sanded (Fig. 3-6).

- **Clothes pins**—the tips of wooden ones can be modified to suit shape of model.
- **Hair clips** (coiffure clips)—metal or plastic.
- **C-clamps**—small sizes.
- **Pins**—straight pins, ball pins, push pins, map tacks.
- **Tweezers**—straight or curved tips; keep them clean of glue.

MEASURING TOOLS

Rulers, a carpenter's square or try square, and calipers are the basic measuring tools needed. Since these tools are often used with knives and saws we recommend they be made out of metal (Fig. 3-7).

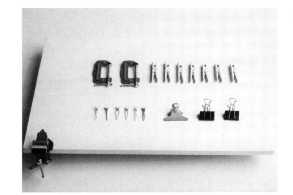

3-6. A plywood building board with a small vise affixed to it. Holding and clamping tools (top to bottom, left to right): C-clamps, clothes pins, hair clips, paper clamps.

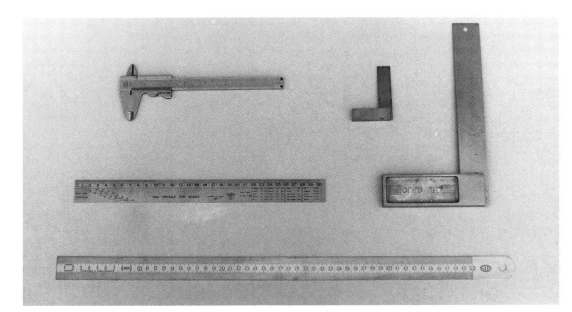

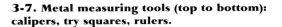

3-7. Metal measuring tools (top to bottom): calipers, try squares, rulers.

ADHESIVES

When wood is used in combination with other materials, the glue chosen must be compatible with all surfaces to be bonded (Fig. 3-8).

White glue—can be used for most jobs; pieces must be clamped or weighed down during drying period.

Balsa cement—dries faster than white glue, making it particularly good for gluing small pieces that need to be handled immediately. Care is required since balsa cement dries glossy and therefore is quite visible on wood.

Epoxy—for structural parts that have small contact areas (chair and table legs, levers, beams); a very strong glue, but using it is more complex than white glue.

A very high bonding strength can be obtained only with long-setting epoxy glues; quick-setting epoxy is not as strong.

FINISHERS

The purpose of fillers and sealers is to ready the wood for painting.

FILLERS

Fillers, no matter what type, do not magically settle into and level out gaps, marks, and grain. Rather, surface tension causes it to stretch over the rough surface with almost uniform thickness. Wood grain will still be apparent after a few coats of filler are applied, which is why sanding between coats is required.

Spackle—basically plaster; being water-based, it must be applied in very small quantities and in very thin layers, particularly on balsa wood. Due to its water content, excess filler will warp the wood.

Polyester fillers—formulated for auto bodywork; harder than spackle. Should not be used to fill small isolated areas, but to coat the whole surface; this is particularly important when applying on balsa.

SEALERS

Sealers help to fill the wood grain and prevent substances that are applied later from penetrating the wood surface. Two types are suitable for wood used in model-making; both are available in spray cans.

Clear dope—may be used under paint or on surfaces to be left unpainted.

Primer—thicker and fill better than clear dope, but because they are colored (gray, red, or yellow), they cannot be used on wood that must have a natural finish.

3-8. An international selection of glues for wood: balsa cements (left); white glues (center); epoxies (right).

PAINT

We recommend spray paints for all applications. Unlike brush paints, they will not leave brush marks. Spray cans are also more practical than spray guns, which need to be cleaned (both the jar and the nozzle), are expensive, and tend to create a lot of mess.

The only problem with using spray cans is the limited choice of colors available. If it is necessary to match the colors on two separate parts of a model and it is impossible to find the right color, it may be better to decide on a marked distinction between the colors.

Using glossy paint is a risk: any minor surface imperfection will be clearly visible. Whenever it is possible, use matte paints and if they are not available, spray a final coat of clear matte finish over the glossy color.

WORKING WITH WOOD

CUTTING

It is more important to consider grain direction when cutting wood than when cutting paper. Before cutting the wood it is important to know whether the cut will be parallel, inclined, or perpendicular to the grain. Parallel cuts present no problems. With inclined cuts the grain tends to drive the blade, like a rail, in a direction that is different from the planned one. Perpendicular cuts are hard to make because there is the risk of breaking the wood along the end of the cut. Two cutting procedures must be considered: with a knife and with a saw.

Using a knife—Select a blade according to the thickness and hardness of the wood: The thinner and softer the wood, the thinner the blade must be. A thick blade tends to deform the wood in the area around the cut (Figs. 3-9, 3-10). An important rule to remember is that it is better to place a little pressure on the knife and to pass it over the same groove repeatedly than it is to use a lot of pressure and to try to cut in one slice. Carefully position a straightedge and hold it firmly while driving the blade along it.

As you approach the end of the cut reduce the pressure on the blade and press hard on the ruler (Fig. 3-11).

A good sharp knife can cut thin hardwood dowels and strips. Cut a dowel by rolling it under the blade. On square and rectangular strips, lightly cut into the wood on all four sides before cutting through the wood strip. This procedure ensures a precise right-angle cut and prevents the wood from breaking off and leaving an uneven edge.

Using a saw—The first thing to take into account is the thickness, or kerf, of the blade. The kerf of a saw blade is the total width of its teeth; in other words, the slice of wood that will disappear as it is "eaten" by the saw. The kerf must be figured in

3-9 *(far left).* **Using a thin blade to cut into a thin balsa strip.**

3-10. **A thick blade deforms soft wood (balsa) in the area around the cut.**

when a piece of wood to be sawn is measured and marked. Select a narrow kerf for soft wood and precision jobs.

A typical beginner's mistake is to force the saw when sawing hard wood; this will only make sawing more difficult. The weight of the saw is almost always sufficient to cut through the wood. The length of the sawing stroke should be as near as possible to the length of the saw. The final strokes should be taken slowly and firmly, and with one hand the waste piece should be held so that the wood does not split on the last stroke (Fig. 3-12).

To obtain a precise cut on hardwood strips, lightly cut into the wood on all four sides before cutting through (Fig. 3-13).

3-11. The result of applying too much pressure to the knife when cutting across the grain of soft wood.

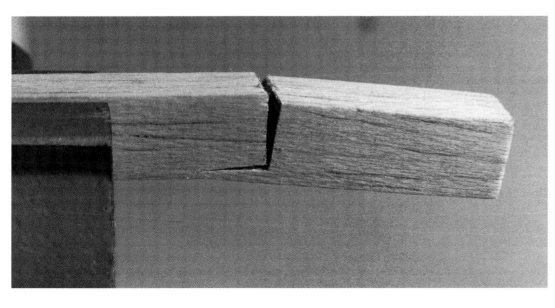

3-12. The consequence of forcing the saw when taking the last strokes.

3-13. Preliminary cuts on all four sides of a hardwood strip to ensure a precise final cut.

MAKING A ROUND SHAPE

This procedure applies only to small parts or details made out of wood. For large objects with round shapes we suggest using expanded resins.

Select a wood strip with a section into which the round shape can be included. If the piece is small and the radiuses are also small, a hardwood is a better choice than balsa because the finishing job will be faster. Draw the plan of the shape onto the piece of wood. Cut it out with a knife or, if you are using hardwood or thick balsa, a saw.

Bevel the edges with a file. Check the dimension of the bevel, which must be inferior to the radius you want to obtain.

Round the beveled edge with abrasive paper (60- to 100-grit, depending on the hardness of the wood and the amount you must remove). Finish the surface using 200- or 300-grit abrasive paper (Fig. 3-14).

Finally, check the radiuses and shape using negative paper templates (Figs. 3-15, 3-16).

3-14. Four-step procedure for making a small round shape. Left to right: piece of wood, cut out; with beveled edges after filing; with beveled, rounded edges; after finishing with 200- or 300-grit abrasive paper.

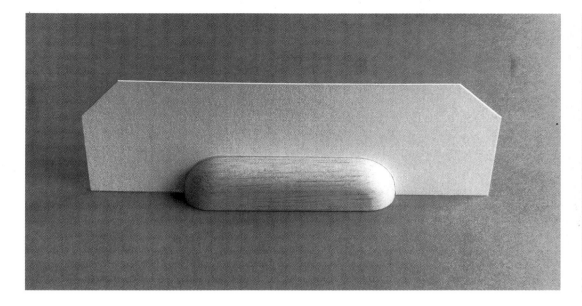

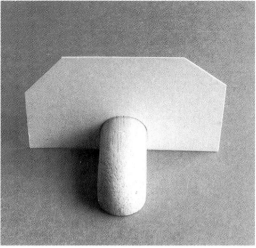

3-15 *(left)*, 3-16. Checking the shape and radiuses with paper templates.

ASSEMBLING AND GLUING

When assembling the parts of the model, it is always important to use some type of guide (assembly plan, braces, try squares) in order to reproduce the geometry you had in mind. Assembling without such guides results in a distorted model; although the geometry may look correct from one angle, when the model is seen from 360 degrees, all assembly imperfections become evident.

If a drawing is used as an assembly plan do not glue the pieces directly over the plan. Instead place a sheet of polyethylene between the drawing and the parts to be glued or rub a candle over the drawing to coat it with wax. This will prevent damage to the model by having the assembly plan permanently stuck to it.

We recommend providing temporary braces to maintain the geometry of the model while glue is setting. If existing triangles or squares cannot meet the requirements of the model's geometry, braces can be made out of foamcore or plywood (Fig. 3-17).

Aside from the properties of the glue itself, two factors are of major importance when gluing: maximizing the contact surfaces and eliminating the interference (dirt, dampness) between the glue and the surfaces to be glued. The heavier and harder the materials to be bonded, the more important these rules become. Paper, for instance, is relatively easy to bond; metal is more difficult. Some glues, such as white glue, are easy to use and allow a range of minor mistakes; others, such as epoxy, require more accuracy.

Where it is possible, the joints of pieces that are subject to some stress should be reinforced with an extra curb of glue; this can be made only after the joint is set and the first application of glue is dry (Fig. 3-18). If the glued pieces will be under a lot of stress do not rely on glue alone to hold the joint together. Provide an extra support system that will work with the glue, such as pins or interlocking joints.

3-17. Providing temporary supports to maintain the geometry of a chair scale model while glue is setting. Supports were made from $^1/_{16}$-inch (1.5mm) cardboard.

3-18. Reinforcing a joint with an extra curb of glue.

FILLING AND SEALING

It is usually better to fill and seal before assembling. A partial exception to this is when parts of a model are connected by a soft, continuous surface; in this case, fill and seal the separate parts and then fill the connecting line or surface.

To effectively provide a smooth surface for painting, multiple coats of filler must be applied and the filler must be sanded almost entirely off between each coat (Figs. 3-19, 3-20). The filler should be softer than the surrounding material; otherwise it will be left after sanding, while the surrounding material will have been sanded down even further.

After filling all gaps, or the whole surface if the wood is very grainy, sand the surface with progressively finer grits of papers (100 to remove filler, 200, 300, and 400 to obtain a smooth surface).

When working with soft wood, such as balsa, the large spots that have been filled can usually still be seen after painting. Coating the entire surface with sealer will overcome this.

Remove all the dust before applying a light coat of sealer. When the sealer is dry, sand again with 400-grit abrasive paper before applying a second coat of sealer. Give it a final sanding with 400- or 500-grit abrasive paper before painting.

Although this procedure may seem long and complex it does not run counter to the philosophy of this book because it is suggested only for details and small parts.

PAINTING

If sealing and filling have been done properly, painting will be easy. Perhaps ninety percent of the surface quality is apparent before the paint is applied. What you see before painting is what you will get afterward; paint will not cover mistakes.

Painting is a messy job and inhaling paint fumes can be harmful. If possible, paint outside, but never when it is very humid or windy, and do not paint in direct sunlight.

Before starting to paint, plan where to position and how to hold the model. It is often possible to make a small hole or to stick nails into the less visible areas of the model, and then hang it with a piece of wire. Never hold the piece to be painted with your hands, even if it is very small.

Remember that wood must *always* be sanded before painting, even if several coats of paint have already been applied.

Thoroughly remove all dust from the surface of the model. Before starting to spray, test the paint on a less visible part of the model to check the quality of the paint, its dilution, and any possible reaction of the sealer. Remember to shake the can very well, at least for one full minute, or more.

Spray cans have modest pressure compared to an air compressor, and as a consequence the paint is very diluted. A lot of paint is needed to properly cover a surface with color. The best results are obtained with many light coats instead of a few heavy ones. The rule is five to six thin coats, though some colors, like yellow and orange,

3-19. Balsa wood surface before filler has been applied.

3-20. Filler applied to a grainy wood (balsa). After sanding, the grain is still apparent but the wood surface is perfectly smooth.

may require extra coats. Runs and sags are the most common consequences of heavy coats of paint and are extremely difficult to remove. After two coats the paint should still be transparent and it should be possible to see the underlying surface.

Allow each coat to dry fully and sand the surface with 400-grit abrasive paper before spraying the next coat. Sometimes marks that were not properly filled become more visible after the first coat. Sanding between coats will help to solve this problem.

If you run out of color, do not switch to a different brand of paint.

As an alternative to the painted abrasive paper technique described under Special Effects in Chapter 1, textured finishes (photoengraving on plastic and special textured paints) can be imitated by first spraying a coat of spray adhesive and following it with the usual coats of paint. Which procedure to use depends on the materials at hand and the quality of grain desired for the texture. Painted abrasive paper renders a grainier texture than painted adhesive (Fig. 3-21).

3-21. Three types of painted surfaces (left to right): glossy; matte; imitation photoengraving, using spray adhesive as a primer.

⬚ ⬚ ⬚ **METAL**

We use metal as a complementary material. Like wood, large and thick metal sheets, tubes, and bars require heavy equipment and a professional workshop.

We rarely use any but the thinnest and softest sheet metal. Unless the metal serves a structural purpose in the model, we prefer to simulate sheet metal with paper covered with metallic adhesive foil. The small size and number of metals we do work with is consistent with our quick and easy approach to model-making (Fig. 4-1).

4-1. Metal for model-making: left, top to bottom—aluminum tubing, brass wire and tubing, piano and iron wire; right, top to bottom—aluminum, copper, and brass sheets.

MATERIALS

Piano wire—high-quality high-carbon steel wire generally employed to make springs for industrial use; can be bought at model shops. The diameters most commonly used in model-making are between $\frac{1}{64}$ and $\frac{1}{16}$ inch (0.4–1.5mm). Larger diameters are available but they are very difficult to bend and unnecessary for our types of models. We use piano wire for aesthetic and structural details; when larger diameters are needed we prefer to use iron, aluminum, brass, or plastic wire.

Brass and aluminum wire—available at model shops; softer than steel wire, can be cut and bent more easily. Brass wire is available in diameters up to $\frac{5}{64}$ inch (2mm); aluminum up to $\frac{1}{8}$ inch (3mm).

Iron wire—soft and very easy to bend; especially good for check models and for visually experimenting with different shapes because it easily can be bent and restraightened. Available in hardware stores. Can be used as a substitute for piano wire; however it is difficult to obtain true straight lines and curves with precise radiuses.

For our purposes, the best type of iron wire is zinc-coated; we generally use diameters ranging from $\frac{1}{16}$ to $\frac{1}{8}$ inch (1.5–3mm).

Aluminum and brass tubing—available at model shops in small diameters (from $\frac{3}{32}$ to $\frac{1}{2}$ inch/2–12mm). Generally used to imitate steel tube in scale models, especially when mechanical or structural realism is needed (e.g., telescopic joints). It is easier to find round tubes than other profiles, but occasionally square, oval, and rectangular profiles can be found at some of the larger shops.

Aluminum, brass, and copper sheets—small sheets (6 by 12 inches/150–300mm) suitable for model-making are available in hobby shops. Aluminum sheets usually range from $\frac{1}{64}$ to $\frac{3}{32}$ inch (0.4–2mm) thick. Brass and copper are harder and come in thinner sheets, rarely exceeding $\frac{1}{16}$ inch (1.5mm).

Expanded metal, perforated metal, welded mesh, metal screening—used to add realism to a model; for example, as speaker panels, grilles, dish drainers and racks, metal baskets, containers, and storage units (Fig. 4-2). Except for metal screening, which can be found in any hardware store, the other materials may be hard to find. Look in the Yellow Pages under metal specialties.

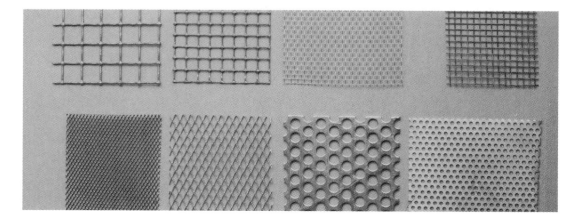

4-2. Metal meshes and screens (top to bottom, left to right): welded mesh; metal screening; expanded metal; perforated metal.

Tools

CUTTING TOOLS

Jeweler's saw—similar to a hacksaw, but better suited for sawing small items, such as tubes, aluminum rods, and profiles.

Diagonal pliers—despite the name, this is a cutting tool; for cutting wire and small rods. A small pair will cut through a maximum of $3/64$ inch (1mm) of steel; medium pliers up to $5/64$ inch (2mm). It is possible to cut softer metal rods with larger diameters.

Snips—for cutting light sheet metal (steel, up to $1/32$ inch/0.7mm thick; aluminum, up to $1/16$ inch/1.5mm thick), expanded metal, perforated metal, welded mesh, and metal screening. Never use snips to cut wire because the blades will be damaged.

Awl—a good-quality, medium-sized awl can be used for marking metal sheets for cuts and the centers of holes to be drilled. An improper, but handy use of an awl (provided it is a good-quality tool) is for cutting aluminum and thin brass sheets ($1/64$ inch/0.4mm).

SHAPING TOOLS

Files—for evening and smoothing out rough edges on sheet metal, tubes, rods, and wire. A high-quality set of small files such as used with wood (see Chapter 3) is suitable for metal as well (Fig. 4-3).

Pliers—for holding and gripping small articles in situations where it may be inconvenient or impossible to use the hands; duck-bill or side-cutting pliers are suited to

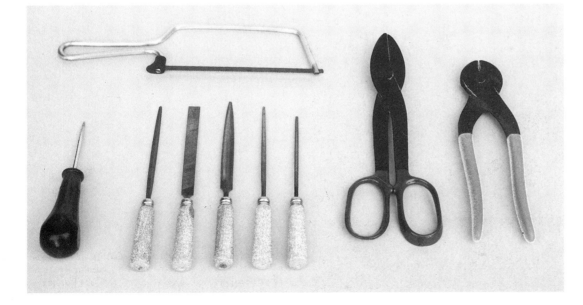

4-3. Some metal-working tools: (top) jeweler's saw; (left to right) awl, set of small files, snips, diagonal pliers.

this use. Side-cutting pliers can also be used for cutting small diameter wire. For bending wire and forming loops, round-nose pliers are indispensable: Other types of pliers will never make a real loop, or a circle, but rather a polygonal form that echoes the form of the pliers nose.

Hammer—like pliers, a universal tool; handy for bending thick wire and, together with other equipment, sheet metal. Choose a small hammer ($\frac{1}{2}$ pound/200–250g).

Drills—portable power drills, standard size and miniature drills. Drills should come equipped with an electronic speed reducer, which is now a standard feature on most modern drills. It is particularly necessary when working with metal. Follow this rule: The bigger the drill bit, the slower the speed. Excessive motor speeds will immediately blunt the bit and render it useless for making the hole.

When making holes over $\frac{1}{3}$ inch (8mm) in the thin sheet metals used for model-making it is better to drill a smaller hole and to achieve the desired diameter with a round file. This avoids the risk of deforming the edge of the hole with the drill bit (Fig. 4-4).

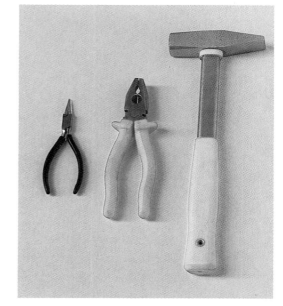

4-4. Some metal-working tools; left to right: round nose pliers; common pliers; hammer.

STRAIGHTEDGES AND MEASURING TOOLS

The same metal rulers and squares as were recommended for wood are suitable for work with metal.

HOLDING AND CLAMPING TOOLS

Vise—attached to a plywood building board such as used for woodworking (see Chapter 3).

Grooved wooden blocks—to be inserted between jaws of vise; the grooves allow a piece of metal tubing to be held fast in the vise without becoming deformed (Fig. 4-5).

4-5. Vise with wooden inserts for holding tubes.

Plywood sheets, hardwood blocks—for sandwiching sheet metal when held in vise during bending process; for pressing against sheet metal as a bending tool.

Miscellaneous—C-clamps, paper clamps, clothes pins, and hair clips are all handy.

CLEANING MATERIALS

Trichloroethylene—to thoroughly clean and remove any grease from metal surfaces to be bonded, whether with glue or solder; other similar dry cleaning fluids are also suitable. All should be used carefully and in a well-ventilated area since they are highly flammable and their fumes are harmful if inhaled.

Abrasive paper—for sanding metal surfaces before and after cleaning in preparation for gluing or soldering. Depending on the situation, the following grits can be used: 200, 280–300, 400, 600.

ADHESIVES

The choice of adhesive depends on the nature of the bond required (high-strength, flexible, quick-setting). Metal, being heavy and not porous, is difficult to glue, and the joints need to be much stronger than with wood or paper (Fig. 4-6). The strongest bond of all is produced by soldering, a more complex and difficult technique than gluing that requires additional equipment.

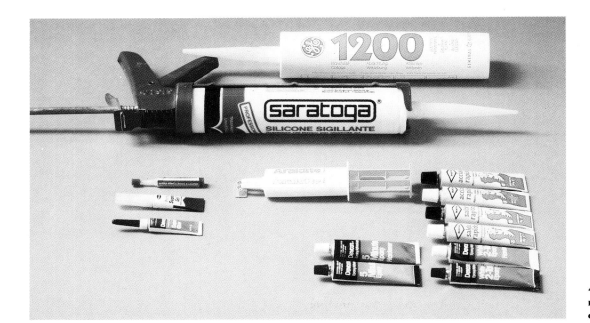

4-6. An international selection of glues for metal: silicone sealant (top); cyanoacrylates; epoxies (left to right).

GLUES

Epoxy—Long-setting epoxies are generally stronger than quick-setting ones. When bonding metals this distinction must be followed with great attention. Use quick-setting epoxies only when a glued piece must be ready immediately for the other steps of the model-building process and when the joint will not be subject to a lot of stress.

Cyanoacrylate—Super or Krazy Glue; an instant-drying glue that provides a very strong bond when used properly. Because this glue sets in a few seconds, pieces can be held with the hands while the glue is drying. The drawback of cyanoacrylate is that it cannot fill gaps and therefore the surfaces to be glued must perfectly mate. Metal parts to be joined must be filed down to provide the maximum possible surface contact without any air gaps. Use in minimum quantities, otherwise the setting time lengthens and the resulting bond is weak.

Silicone sealant—not a real glue; can be used to form an elastic, though not strong, bond between large pieces; it functions as a filler between uneven surfaces, closing up air gaps. Silicone is a messy material; we suggest using it only on parts that will not be visible.

SOLDERING EQUIPMENT

Electric soldering iron—Among the many different tools for soldering, the electric soldering iron is a good compromise between price and performance. The main feature of a good soldering iron is its power; it should have no less than 150 watts, but the ideal is a 200-watt iron.

Solder—a tin-lead alloy that should contain no less than 50 percent tin; use solder without rosin core.

Soldering acid—cleans the metal so that the solder can bond to it; available in liquid or paste; the paste is easier to find, but the fluid does a better job of getting into tight spots.

Sal ammoniac—for deoxidizing the tip of the soldering iron when hot. Being pure copper, the tip oxidizes when it is heated and the oxide acts as an insulator. If sal ammoniac is not available, sand the tip until it is shiny, then apply a drop of soldering acid to it (Fig. 4-7).

FINISHERS

PRIMER AND PAINT

In principle, all metal should be primed before painting. However, the purposes of priming are protection against corrosion, for objects that must stay outdoors, and increasing the grip of paints on the surface of metallic objects that must be handled

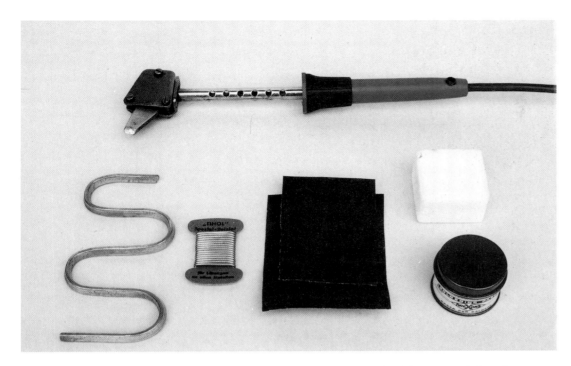

4-7. Soldering equipment: electric soldering iron (top); solders, abrasive paper, sal ammoniac block, soldering paste (left to right).

as they are used. Because neither of these purposes is applicable to model-making, we can therefore say that priming is largely unnecessary.

Use the normal spray cans, usually available at hardware stores. These are general-purpose paints and can be used on both wood and metal.

CUTTING

Using a saw—Use the saw to cut tubes, small rods, and similar items. Place the material to be cut in a vise and position the layout line just outside of the vise jaw so that the piece will not vibrate under the saw's action. Again, never force the saw, but make long, light strokes. Saw approximately one fourth of the whole section, then reposition the piece in the vise by rotating it ninety degrees and saw another fourth. By doing this four times, you will cut through the entire section and obtain a precise cut.

Using snips—Use snips only for light gauge metal. We suggest avoiding big work with metal, such as large sheets or heavy gauge sheet metal. Consider whether a surrogate material, such as paper, can do the job and save time.

Snips will not remove any metal when a cut is made on sheet metal. For this reason, the edges of the sheet will be deformed and minute fractures will be produced by the shearing process. We therefore suggest cutting just outside of the layout line so that it will be possible to file down the edge while staying within the required dimensions.

To make straight cuts, place the sheet metal on a board with the marked guideline outside the edge; hold the sheet firmly with one hand and hold the snips so that the flat sides of the blades are at right angles to the surface to be cut; inclined blades will produce bent and burred edges.

When cutting out a shape, cut away most of the extra material outside the layout line and leave a narrow piece to be cut off later. This will allow the extra material to curl up below the blades of the snips and the scrap will be out of the way while you cut. Always finish the cut with a file (Figs. 4-8, 4-9).

Complex shapes can be cut in a similar way: First make a rough cut; get closer to the desired outline with a second cut; refine the cut with the file.

Using an awl—Straight cuts can be precisely executed on thin sheet metal with a sharp awl. Mark the sheet on *both* sides where it has to be cut; then pass the awl over the cutting lines many times, on both sides. The sheet will eventually become grooved and then can be neatly separated by bending along the groove. File all cut edges (Fig. 4-10).

Using diagonal pliers—To obtain a neat cut, partially cut a piece of wire while rotating it 360 degrees, rather than cutting straight through the wire in a single cut. A single cut through the wire will produce a chisel point instead of a flush edge.

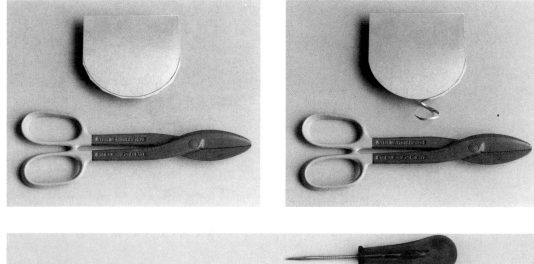

4-8 (far left). Cutting sheet metal with a pair of snips. Cutting outside the layout line avoids deforming the sheet's edges.

4-9. Cutting sheet metal with a pair of snips. The scrap curls up below the blades of the snips and does not hinder cutting.

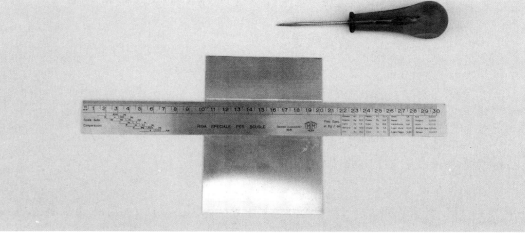

4-10. Cutting a sheet of aluminum with an awl and a ruler.

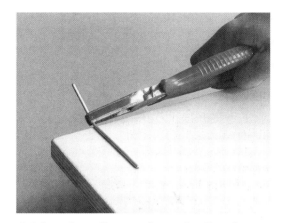

4-11. Using pliers against a hard surface to make a sharp bend in a piece of piano wire.

Bending wire—Use pliers to hold one end of wire to be bent. If a sharp bend between two straight lines is required, push the other end against a hard, flat surface (building board, metal ruler). Holding that end with the fingers will produce a slightly bowed, rather than straight, bend (Figs. 4-11, 4-12).

Bending tubing—A typical industrial technique requiring specialized equipment. It is, however, possible to bend brass or aluminum tubing of diameters no greater than ⅓ inch (8mm). They should be relatively thick compared to their diameter (1/32–3/64 inch/0.8–1mm). The procedure is difficult but in some circumstances may be justified. Aside from the physical challenge of bending metal tubing, the main problem to be overcome when specialized equipment is not used is that the tubing becomes oval in the bent area. In other words, the cross section at the bend is wider and flatter than the original section. This undesirable effect can be corrected with a specially built form adapter or mold (Fig. 4-13).

This device can be made by cutting three pieces of plywood to a curve that corresponds to the desired radius of the tubing when bent. Form a sandwich with the middle board recessed a distance equal to two-thirds of the tube's diameter; nail or screw the three pieces together. The angle formed by the two straight sides of the mold must be slightly inferior to the angle that will be formed by the two arms of the tube.

All metals have a "memory"; therefore, after bending, the tube will try to resume its original shape. Thus the angle of the mold must be a bit narrower to compensate for this tendency.

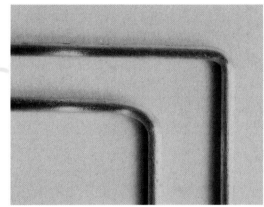

4-12. The right way: a straight, sharp bend made with pliers against a board (top). The wrong way: a bowed bend made with pliers and the free hand (bottom).

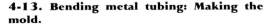

4-13. Bending metal tubing: Making the mold.

Clamp the mold into the vise and position the tube in the mold's slot (Fig. 4-14). Use a block of hardwood to slowly push the tube to follow the contour of the mold. In some cases, hammering may help (Fig. 4-15).

Once the bend is made, use a cardboard template or a protractor to check the angle obtained (Fig. 4-16). If the angle needs to be corrected do not try to do so by hand. You will merely deform the tube at the bend and it will have to be discarded. Instead, correct the curve of the mold and repeat the bending operation.

Clearly this is a difficult procedure, one we do not recommend for tubing of hard metals or with large diameters. Plastic dowels and tubes should be used instead (see Chapter 5).

Bending sheets—A procedure that is, in principle, similar to the industrial technique of bending sheet metal and, therefore, like many other procedures described in this book, will show the designer the potential, limitations, and difficulties of similar manufacturing processes.

Place the sheet to be bent between two pieces of plywood or hardwood as wide as or wider than the metal sheet. Since the bend will be made against one of the boards, the part of the sheet to be bent must extend beyond the edges of the wood. If the bend is to be sharp, the edge of the board must also be sharp; if the bend is to have a specific radius, the edge of one of the boards must be curved to match that radius.

Clamp the wood-metal-wood sandwich in the vise; if the assemblage is more than three times wider than the vise jaws, add C-clamps to each extremity to keep the sandwich tightly closed.

With a third block of hardwood or thick piece of plywood, slowly press the part of metal sheet that extends from the wooden boards. Try to keep the wood block parallel to the edges of the two boards (Figs. 4-17, 4-18).

When making a sharp bend with thick sheets it is particularly important to apply pressure very slowly; otherwise the metal may tear. The best way to do this is to proceed in small steps, allowing the structure of the metal to adjust after each push.

If the metal is very hard it may be necessary to exert more force by striking it with a hammer. Never hit metal directly; always place a block of wood between the hammer and the metal sheet.

4-14. Bending metal tubing: Positioning the piece of tube.

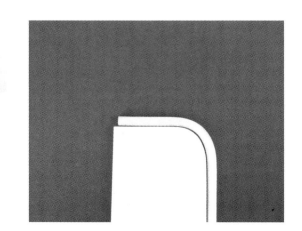

4-15 *(far left)*. Bending metal tubing: The completed bend.

4-16. Bending metal tubing: Checking the angle with a cardboard template.

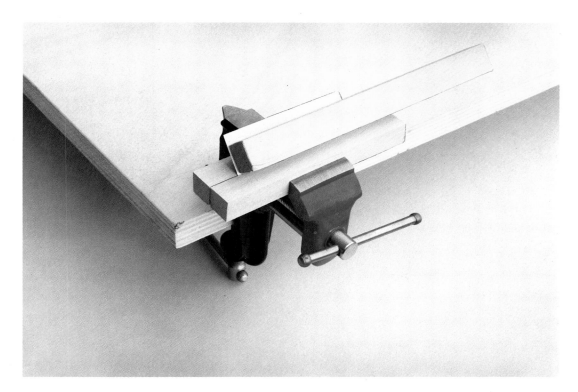

4-17. Bending a sheet of aluminum: Making a sharp bend against a right-angle edge.

4-18. Bending a sheet of aluminum: Making a soft bend against a curved edge.

DRAWING

Drawing is a technique related to bending that involves forming metal into a hollow shape with a punch that forces it into the cavity of a die. It can be used to make realistic looking models for grilles on speakers, air intakes, and exhausts. (Please note that the minimal equipment we use is capable of drawing metal *screening* only; to draw sheet metal, industrial equipment is needed.)

The procedure begins with making a simple wooden mold that will act as a punch and die.

Using a jigsaw, cut out the shape of the grille from a piece of ½-inch (12mm) plywood. The path left by the saw serves as the interspace between the punch and the die. The metal screening must fit in this space when the wooden mold is closed. Therefore, it is sometimes necessary to widen the interspace by filing down the edge of either the punch or the die. The edge of the punch must have a radius that corresponds to the desired radius of the grille's rim.

Use snips to cut a piece of screening that is larger than the die; the extra material is necessary for the wall of the grille and for drawing the screening into the mold (see Fig. 4-19).

Attach the punch to the building board with nails and lay the piece of metal screening on it; place the die on top of the two. Use a hammer to lightly tap all around the die. This will force together the two halves of the mold, drawing the metal screening into the interspace that separates the die from the punch (Fig. 4-20).

Open the mold (separate the punch from the die) and pull out the shaped grille (Fig. 4-21). Trim off excess material with scissors or snips (depending on the screen's thickness).

GLUING

Bonding metal is a tough job for a glue to perform. Because metal is not porous it offers a reduced surface onto which glue can adhere compared to wood and paper. Furthermore, the greater weight of metal places a lot of stress on the joint, increasing the difficulty of achieving a strong bond.

Cleaning the surfaces—Thoroughly cleaning surfaces to be joined is of capital importance when working with metal. Metal is often oily, and any trace of oil or dirt left on the surfaces will weaken the joint. New piano wire may look clean, but it has a rustproof coating that must be removed before gluing.

The best way to clean metal surfaces is with trichloroethylene or similar dry cleaning product. Work in a well-ventilated area: These substances are highly flammable and their fumes are noxious.

After degreasing all surfaces to be bonded, sand them with 200-grit abrasive paper. Clean all surfaces again with trichloroethylene. After cleaning the metal for the last time do not touch it anymore with your fingers. Use a pair of pliers or tweezers to handle the wire.

4-19. Drawing metal screening: Plywood punch (left) and die (right); oversize piece of screening is in foreground.

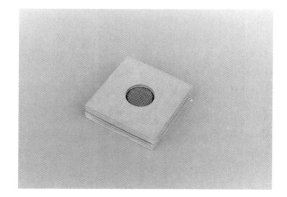

4-20. Drawing metal screening: The punch-and-die assembly is pressed or tapped together, drawing the screening into the desired shape.

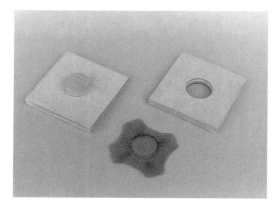

4-21. Drawing metal screening: The punch-and-die assembly is opened. Note the shape obtained by drawing; excess material has not yet been trimmed off.

Making a difficult bond—For example, gluing a short piece of wire to a small piece of sheet metal. This type of bond can be quite troublesome because the contact surface of the two pieces is very narrow and the wire acts as a lever, exerting great force over the joint. Epoxy is the best adhesive to use in a case like this.

The first step is to increase the contact surface; one solution is to bend the wire twice at right angles (about ½ inch/12mm each arm) where it will be glued to sheet metal (Fig. 4-22), providing the wire with a base on which to stand in an upright position.

A double goal can be achieved by sanding the surfaces to be glued: The metal's surface is cleaned, and the surface becomes coarser. Remember that a coarse metal surface means more surface for the glue to adhere to.

Mix the epoxy with the hardener and spread it with a stick over the contact area on both the metal sheet and the wire. It is advisable to reinforce the joint with a second application of glue after the first bond has set. When working in a hurry or when it is necessary to proceed with the construction of the model, use a quick-setting epoxy for the first bond and a long-setting one for the reinforcement.

Epoxy glues will set faster and the bond will be much stronger if the hardening reaction takes place at relatively high temperatures (80°–200°F/26°–94°C). If the joint is steady enough to be transported without glue (never count on glue as a connecting or structural element before it has completely dried), the piece can be left to set in a kitchen oven. If this is not possible, place a lamp very close to the bond; the heat produced by the bulb will raise the temperature of the joint at least to the recommended minumum.

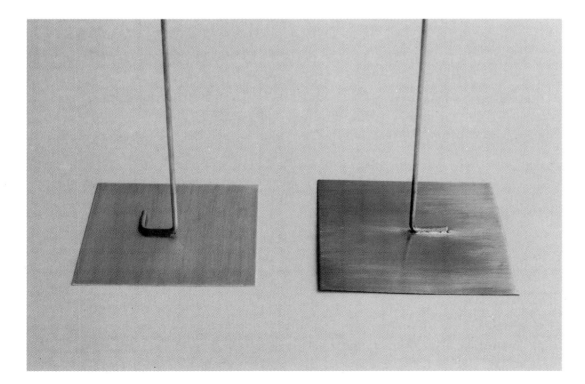

4-22. A comparison between two wire-to-sheet metal bonds: epoxy (left) and solder (right). Note the larger contact area of the joint at left.

Soldering produces stronger joints than gluing. It can be used on all metals used for model-making except aluminum or stainless steel. It is, however, a more complex and difficult technique and it requires some extra equipment. Resort to solder when the joint between two metal parts must be particularly strong or when it is impossible to provide enough contact surface to glue the two pieces.

The superior bond obtained with soldering requires that the procedure be done absolutely correctly. The surface must be scrupulously cleaned, following the three steps outlined for gluing (cleaning with trichloroethylene, sanding, and cleaning again). After cleaning, the surfaces to be soldered must not be touched with the hands.

Solder can make a bond between two surfaces only if it is in a liquid state. The job of the soldering iron is to heat the surfaces sufficiently to liquefy the solder.

In order to convey the maximum heat to the surfaces of the joint, the soldering iron must be free of oxide and the contact time between the soldering iron and the surfaces to be soldered should be long enough for the heat to be completely transferred from the iron to the surfaces.

Finally, the solder must flow precisely between the surfaces to be bonded.

If all the above principles are observed, the soldering process is relatively simple and will be successful. Position and steady the parts to be joined by means of the appropriate holding tools (C-clamps, paper clamps, clothes pins). If you are using masking tape, do not place it too close to the bonding area or the heat will melt the adhesive.

After thoroughly cleaning the surfaces, use a toothpick or small brush to apply some soldering acid to both surfaces on the spots where the solder will go. Heat the surfaces to be soldered by holding the tip of the soldering iron to them. Some of the acid will evaporate; do not breathe the fumes. To ensure that both surfaces are at the same temperature, move the iron evenly along both of them.

When the surfaces are hot enough, apply the solder to them, not to the iron. The sign of adequate heat is that the solder melts and stays liquid as long as the iron is in contact with the surfaces. It should flow evenly over the surfaces, making them look wet.

If the solder melts when it touches the tip of the soldering iron but solidifies as it touches the surfaces, the iron is not hot enough or, more likely, does not have enough power. If the solder beads up and rolls away, either the surfaces are not clean or the metal is unsuitable for soldering—aluminum or stainless steel.

Allow the bond to cool off for a few minutes, wash the area with a sponge to remove the acid residue, and wipe it dry with a paper towel. Remove the excess solder with a small file, but be careful not to damage the bond by filing away too much material.

Metal is used in model-making for structural purposes and to represent metal parts that will have either a chrome or a painted finish.

Chrome—Sand the metal with a relatively coarse abrasive paper (200-grit) and follow with a fine one (600-grit). When the surface is well polished and shiny, stop touching it with your hands. Prop it against a suitable support and spray it with clear lacquer. Use glossy for a shiny finish, matte for a dull one. A clear coating is absolutely necessary to keep the metal from oxidizing within a short period of time.

Paint—To paint metal, use the general-purpose spray cans mentioned earlier in this chapter. Metal must be cleaned, but not necessarily primed, before it can be painted. The procedure prior to painting is similar to the cleaning sequence described for gluing and soldering, but is not as fussy and detailed: Sand the surface with 280–300-grit abrasive paper, degrease it with trichloroethylene, and then start applying paint. Do not sand in between coats; allow the first coat to dry completely before spraying the next one. Because metal does not absorb paint, runs and sags are more likely to occur here than on wood; to avoid this, apply very light coats of paint. Three or four coats are usually enough, since metal has no grain to be covered. Yellow usually requires an extra coat.

5 ▽▽▽ PLASTIC

We use plastic, like metal and wood, as a complementary material. In many cases plastic is easier to work with. It holds an advantage over wood because it is a finished material; any additional finishing, if at all required, is minimal. Compared to metal, plastic is softer, and thus easier to cut, bend, and join.

These advantages notwithstanding, plastic is not universally interchangeable with wood and metal. The choice of materials must take into consideration the size of the model; the feasibility of obtaining the desired shape with one or another material; the intended look; and structural qualities.

Let us take as an example, the design of a chair; the frame will be out of steel tubing. Out of which material should a scale model be built? If the scale is small (1:10) and the diameter of the tubing no greater than $5/8$ inch (15mm), the only reasonable choice is metal. Wood is clearly unsuitable given the shape and look of the model. Plastic is not a good choice because $1/16$-inch (1.5mm) plastic dowels are very hard to find and would be too flexible for a structure like a chair frame. If the scale of the model is larger (1:4), then plastic is the better material, being easier to cut, bend, and glue than metal.

Plastic sheet is increasingly being used in preference to wooden blocks and clay in design schools, design offices, and even in model-makers' workshops. It saves time and effort, is clean to work with, and does not require heavy equipment. Furthermore, precision shaping and finishing are considerably easier. Compared with paper and foam, however, cutting, bonding, and gluing plastic are more complex processes. Exclusive use of plastic requires a real workshop with at least a drill press, bandsaw, and lathe, in contrast to the simplicity of the cutting board and handtools we use in working with paper.

Using plastic for details or parts of models, however, falls within the boundaries of our quick and easy approach. More extensive use of this material is a valid option for model-making but should be considered in light of the greater time and equipment requirements involved.

MATERIALS

The plastic materials that we use, while chemically different, have similar characteristics. Perhaps the only exception is clear acetate sheet, which is very much like paper: Cut with scissors or mat knife, glued with its specific glue or with Scotch tape (see Adhesives section later in this chapter).

Today there is a great number of plastic resins on the market but not all are available in the shapes and sizes necessary for model-building. The plastics you are most likely to encounter are polyvinyl chloride (PVC), polymethyl-methacrylate (Plexiglas), acetate, acrylonitrile butadiene styrene (ABS), and polystyrene (Fig. 5-1). Polyethylene and polypropylene are unsuitable for model-making because they are impossible to glue.

Dowels—made of polyvinyl chloride and polymethyl-methacrylate in diameters ranging from $\frac{1}{8}$ to $\frac{1}{2}$ inch (3–12mm) are widely available at model shops; other resins (including polyethylene and polypropylene, which we do not recommend) can be found at plastic supply shops. Larger diameters are also available but they are hard to bend. PVC comes in solid colors; polymethyl-methacrylate is usually clear.

Strips—square, rectangular, and structural sections are occasionally available at model shops. They are sometimes employed in architectural models, but we rarely use them.

Tubing—use only PVC; avoid polypropylene, which is frequently sold instead of PVC. PVC tubing is a typical lumberyard and hardware item, found in a minimum diameter of $\frac{1}{2}$ inch (12mm). Tubes with larger diameters are produced in different thicknesses; occasionally diameters smaller than $\frac{1}{2}$ inch can be found at hobby shops.

Sheets—acetate (usually clear), PVC, ABS, polystyrene, and polymethyl-methacrylate; found in model shops and in specialized plastic supply outlets. Be sure to buy real acetate; many times an aesthetically similar but chemically different product is sold in place of real acetate.

PVC, ABS, polystyrene, polymethyl-methacrylate sheets are usually available in thicknesses ranging from $\frac{1}{32}$ inch (0.8mm) to $\frac{3}{16}$ inch (5mm). We suggest using sheets no thicker than $\frac{1}{8}$ inch (3mm) in order to avoid cutting and bending difficulties. Acetate sheet, an art shop item, is usually available in thicknesses ranging from 0.003 inch (0.08mm) to 0.02 inch (0.5mm). Occasionally, acetate $\frac{3}{64}$ inch (1mm) thick is available.

5-1. A selection of plastics for model-making: sheets—ABS, polystyrene, PVC, clear polymethyl-methacrylate, clear acetate (left, top to bottom); tubing, dowels, strips (right, top to bottom).

Tools

Most of the tools used for working with metal and wood are suitable for plastic as well. For cutting dowels, strips, and tubing, use a jeweler's saw. Snips or a good pair of scissors can be used to cut acetate and thin PVC sheets (maximum 1/32 inch/0.8mm thick). Do not use snips on polymethyl-methacrylate, polystyrene, and ABS; they are more brittle than PVC and acetate, and the snips' blades will chip their edges.

A set of small files; drills; the standard holding and clamping devices, including a vise; and measuring tools are the same as described in Chapter 4. In addition, various pieces of plywood will be needed to make molds. In the event the plastic is painted, fine abrasive paper (400- to 600-grit) and matte-finish spray paints should be used.

The awl can be used to cut all types of plastic sheets, exactly as explained in Chapter 4.

Hot-air gun—a specialized tool for plastic; used for bending sheets, dowels, and tubing. It resembles a hair dryer but is more powerful and produces a more concentrated high-temperature airflow (Fig. 5-2). Nozzles of different shapes can be mounted on the mouth of the gun to direct and concentrate the hot airflow; the flat one is recommended but is not essential for bending plastic sheets.

5-2. Hot-air gun.

Adhesives

The glues used on plastic materials fall into two groups: specific glues for the different resins and all-purpose glues that are also good for plastic (Fig. 5-3).

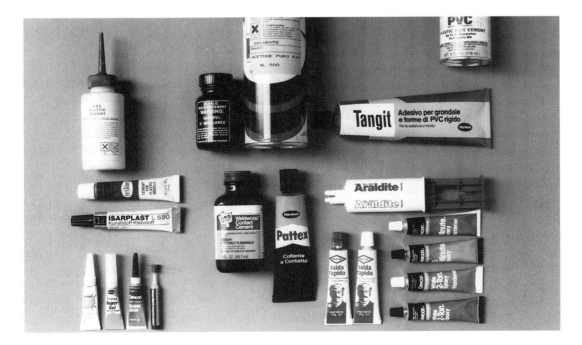

5-3. An international selection of glues for plastics: ABS and polystyrene glues, cyanoacrylates (left, top to bottom); polymethylmethacrylate glue and acetone, contact cements (center, top to bottom); PVC glues, epoxy glues (right, top to bottom).

SPECIFIC RESINS

Special glues are made for PVC, polystyrene, ABS, and polymethyl-methacrylate.

PVC glue—can be found at hardware stores and lumber yards; usually employed for joining and sealing PVC pipes and gutters.

Polystyrene and ABS glues—can be bought at model shops; usually employed for building plastic scale models.

Polymethyl-methacrylate glue—hard to find; some model shops and specialized plastic outlets may carry it.

Clear acetate requires special attention for bonding because most adhesives will be visible when dry. Use adhesives in small quantities.

Acetone (oil-free nail polish remover)—for use only on clear acetate; will not glue other materials, such as PVC or imitation acetate.

Clear polyester tape—will make an almost invisible bond on clear acetate (see Chapter 1).

ALL-PURPOSE GLUES

Epoxy—the only all-purpose glue that can be used on almost every type of plastic resin. Of course, if used on clear polymethyl-methacrylate and on other transparent plastics it will be visible (and ugly). Epoxy should be used for plastic-metal, plastic-wood, and plastic-paper bonds.

Cyanoacrylate—being absolutely transparent, can be used on clear polymethyl-methacrylate and on many other resins. Polystyrene and ABS are chemically attacked by cyanoacrylate, but since this glue is used only in small quantities, its reaction on the plastic will hardly be noticeable. Even in small quantities, it will be visible on clear acetate.

Contact cement—for gluing plastic sheets to plastic or to other materials; should not be used on transparent plastic sheets, because of its strong yellow color, nor on polystyrene and ABS, because it will melt them.

WORKING WITH PLASTIC

CUTTING

Cutting plastic presents no difficulties, largely because it has no grain. Follow the basic cutting rules in Chapter 3 and employ the hints in the Tools section earlier in this chapter.

BENDING

Heat is always required for bending plastic. It is important to work slowly and systematically, taking care not to strain the material. Wait until the material is hot enough. Because the temperature range between solid and molten state is relatively small, however, be careful not to overheat it.

Bending a dowel—This procedure employs a mold and allows for a maximum of two bends, as long as they both lie in the same plane and are not too far away from each other.

To determine the length of dowel needed, make a drawing or sketch of the finished form with the dimensions and radiuses. Cut the piece a little longer than the desired full development.

The mold can be made of foamcore, cardboard, or plywood. We suggest making both the internal and the external part of the mold, so that the dowel will be perfectly guided into its new curved shape.

Mark the extremities of the curve on the dowel. Use masking tape to protect those parts that will not be bent; the tape will shield the straight segments of the dowel from the heat and will also indicate where the dowel should be bent.

Heat the part to be bent with the hot-air gun, taking care not to overheat or to hold the air gun too close to the plastic surface. If the dowel is more than ¼ inch (6mm) in diameter, rotate it as you heat it (Fig. 5-4).

Place the dowel with its soft bends between the two parts of the mold. Make sure the whole dowel is lying on the mold's plane and is properly inserted. Do not hurry; make sure that your piece assumes the shape you have planned for it. If the dowel has been heated thoroughly (all around and for long enough), the plastic will retain the heat for long enough to allow you to work without haste (Figs. 5-5, 5-6).

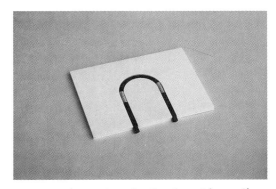

5-5. Bending a dowel: The dowel is cooling off in the mold.

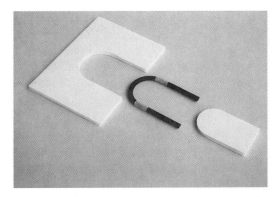

5-6. Bending a dowel: The bent dowel is ready to be cut to size.

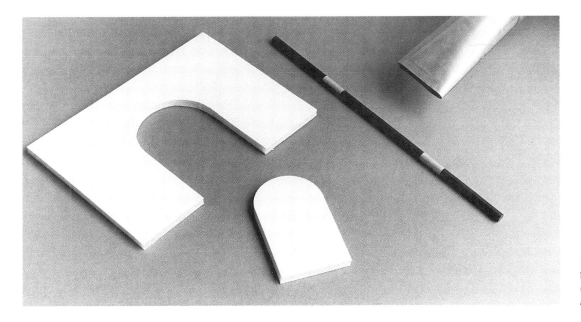

5-4. Bending a dowel: Heating the dowel before placing it in the foamcore mold. Note the masking tape at the extreme ends of the area to be curved.

When the piece has cooled, remove it from the mold and cut to size.

Bending a tube—Select PVC tubing with the thickest possible wall. For example, if the diameter is ¾ inch (20mm), the wall should be ⅛ inch (3mm).

The procedure is similar to that described for dowels, except the mold must be made of plywood or hardwood and the forming equipment must include two more wooden boards to create a sandwich. The board that will lie on the table will hold together the internal and the external part of the mold. The other board will be placed on top of the mold to prevent the tube from being flattened in the bent area. The thickness of the internal and the external parts of the mold must be equal to the diameter of the tube.

The geometric reaction of the plastic tube to the bending force is similar to that of a metal tube (see Chapter 4). However, heat-softening the plastic tube overcomes the opposition to assuming a new shape and causes the tubing almost to flow into its new shape. A lid (the top board) is needed to help this "flowing" by pushing the tube into its mold.

Cut, mark, and mask the tube as described for bending a dowel. Heat it with the hot-air gun, remembering to constantly rotate the tube all the while (Fig. 5-7).

Position the mold over its baseboard, the tubing in the mold, and cover the mold with its lid. After the tube has completely cooled, cut it to size (Fig. 5-8).

Press bending a tube—By making a few modifications to the procedure just described it is possible to imitate press bending, an industrial technique employed to make short-radius bends on tubes characterized by a concave shape in the internal side of the curve. This concave shape is usually called *crimp*.

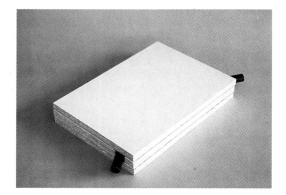

5-8. Bending a tube: The tube enclosed in the mold and pushed into place by the cover.

5-7. Bending a tube: Heating the tube. Note the baseboard and cover for the mold.

Make a small wooden peg with a rounded point; this will act as a ram. The external part of the mold is similar to the one used in bending a tube but the lid and bottom board must be modified by the addition of a guide for the peg. The peg, when inserted into the guide, will function as the internal part of the mold. This will then shape the concavity, or crimp, that characterizes press binding.

Heat the tube as usual and place it into the mold; clamp on the lid and ram in the peg (Fig. 5-9). The peg forces the excess material resulting from bending the tube into a newly created concave shape (Fig. 5-10).

5-9. Press bending a tube: The tube clamped in the mold, the peg rammed into place.

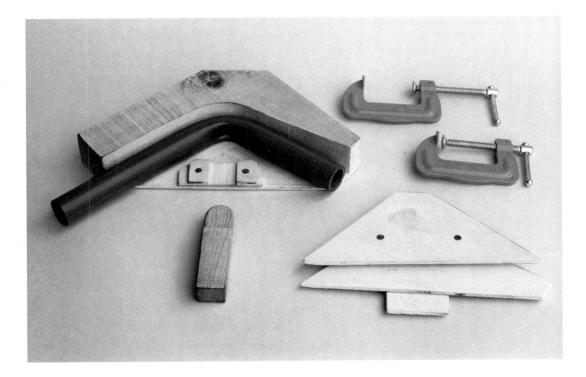

5-10. Press bending a tube: The bent tube. Note the peg and the guides used to ram the tube.

Bending a sheet—The term *bending* does not adequately describe all the potential of this procedure, which allows for the creation of complex shapes as long as the bends or curves have parallel axes. There are some limitations, however. It is not possible to deep-draw the material. This technique cannot be used to make curves with axes lying on different planes since that involves stretching and shrinking the material, which requires a more complex technique called vacuum forming.

Begin by making male and female molds of plywood or hardwood. The dimensions of the mold should be slightly larger than those of the piece to be bent. Allow an extra space, equal to the thickness of the plastic sheet to be bent, between the male and the female parts to be occupied by the plastic sheet.

Cut the sheet a little larger than needed to accommodate the bends and cut it down to size after bending.

Pass the air gun evenly back and forth over the area where the bend will be. Keep the air gun far enough away from the plastic sheet to avoid overheating.

When the sheet is softened, place it in the mold and tighten with C-clamps or screws (Figs. 5-11, 5-12).

5-11. Bending a sheet: The assembled mold. A solid hardwood mold may be so heavy that no clamps are necessary, as in this case.

5-12. Bending a sheet: The molded sheet. Note that multiple bends can be made as long as all lie along the same axis.

An easier method for a simple bend—The procedure just described can be used for compound bends. A simpler mold can be made when only a single bend, such as a dihedral angle, has to be made. If the sheet is no thicker than ⁵⁄₆₄ inch (2mm) make the mold of foamcore bent to correspond to the desired angle. For thicker plastic sheets, make the male part of the mold out of plywood or hardwood; no female part is needed. Cut the sheet larger than needed.

For the best results heat only the line where the bend will be. Mount a nozzle with a wide flat opening on the mouth of the hot-air gun and use two plywood boards to mask the areas of the plastic sheet that will remain flat. The nozzle and the narrow groove between the two wooden boards will concentrate the heat along the bending line (Figs. 5-13, 5-14, 5-15).

5-14. Making a simple bend: The sheet is cooling off on the foamcore mold.

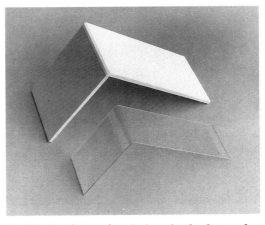

5-15. Making a simple bend: The bent plastic sheet.

5-13. Making a simple bend: Heating the area to be bent; plywood protects all other parts of the sheet.

GLUING

As with metal, all pieces to be glued must be perfectly clean, without any trace of grease or dirt. The safest cleaning agent is soap and water. Although more effective, trichloroethylene will melt ABS and polystyrene, and alcohol may mar the surface of other plastics. Remember that there are thousands of plastic resins, and even those within the same family can have large differences (not all polymethyl-methacrylates are the same, for instance), so it is hard to predict how a given resin will react to a given cleaning agent. A good strategy is to test your cleaner on a scrap piece of the material you are using.

Sanding is also necessary before gluing, to increase the contact surface. Carefully go over areas to be bonded with 400-grit abrasive paper, making sure not to spoil surfaces that will not be glued but will be visible in the finished model.

Glues for plastic sometimes require special procedures; thoroughly follow the directions of the glue you are using. Whenever it is possible, test the glue on a piece of scrap material to determine the glue's resistance and setting time, as well as whether it will cause any reaction with the resin.

Use appropriate clamps to hold glued parts in place while glue sets. If joints will be under a lot of stress, provide extra support as described under Assembling and Gluing in Chapter 3.

FINISHING

We have said that one of the virtues of plastic is that, as a finished material, it does not need to be painted. Because it is difficult to find plastic in other colors besides red, gray, black, and white, however, painting may be necessary to obtain a desired color.

Preparation for painting begins with degreasing the piece by washing it with soap and water. Do not use trichloroethylene or alcohol; aside from marring the plastic, these solvents may damage the glue you have used. Sand all surfaces with very fine abrasive paper (400- to 600-grit) and thoroughly remove all resultant dust. Before applying paint, test a piece of scrap. The surface of some resins, such as polystyrene and ABS, may be marred by the solvents in certain paints.

Painting plastic is the same as for metal: Apply three to four thin coats (remember to add an extra coat for yellow); do not sand between coats.

When gluing plastic, a little bit of glue may sometimes ooze out visibly from the joint or an extra curb of glue may have been added to reinforce the joint. In both cases a very light coat of matching spray paint over the spot will cover the glue; there is no need to prepare the surface. Mask the surrounding area if it is a different color and might be accidentally sprayed.

FABRIC

In Chapter 2 we mentioned that expanded polyethylene and foam rubber can be used to imitate upholstery. When they cannot, particularly in models of heavily stuffed or cushioned armchairs, it is necessary "to upholster" the model with real fabric.

Our method of upholstering models does not involve fitting out furniture following traditional techniques. We have used our "quick and easy" philosophy to reinterpret the long, involved process of upholstering. Apply this method only to small scale models (maximum scale is 1:3). Working in a larger scale requires traditional upholstery methods.

MATERIALS AND SUPPLIES

Fabric—use only lightweight fabrics, such as jacket lining material and cotton shirting. Heavy, textured cloth would be out of scale and would not work well with our technique (Fig. 6-1).

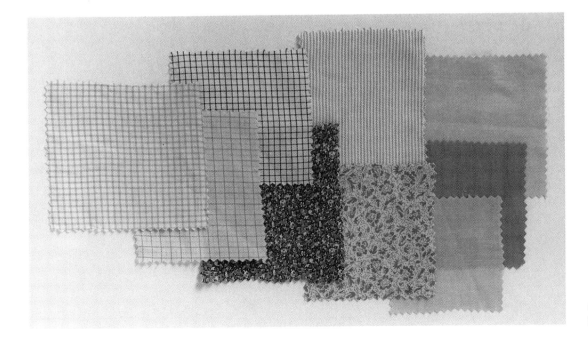

6-1. Samples of thin fabric suitable for upholstering.

Stuffing—for an "office" look, use soft polyurethane foam; for a "home" look, use polyester fiber or cotton batting.

Tools—the tools required for working with fabric are basically the same as those used with paper (see Chapter 1).

Adhesives—the basis of our method is to glue the fabric instead of sewing it. There are glues made particularly for cloth. White glue works equally well, as long as the fabric is not washed after gluing (Fig. 6-2).

UPHOLSTERING

Step-by-step instructions for making a cushion follow. The same procedure can be used for more complex upholstered shapes.

Iron the cloth. Trace the pattern of the cushion onto the reverse side of the fabric, allowing plenty of extra material outside the gluing line, to be trimmed off later. Cut out two identical pieces of fabric.

If the stuffing is polyurethane foam, cut it to size and round all corners with scissors. If you are using cotton or polyester fiber batting, shape and trim it with scissors.

The cushion will be formed with foamcore framing. If the cushion is to be double-convex, build two foamcore frames to press together the margin around the cushion while the glue is drying. If the cushion is plano-convex, only one frame is needed; the margin will be pressed between the foamcore and the work surface.

Different fabrics absorb glue differently. Diluting white glue with a little water will aid absorption. It is a good idea to test the glue you intend to use on a scrap of fabric to see how well it is absorbed and to see if it stains the fabric.

Apply the glue in small dots (see Gluing, Chapter 1) along the seam line to give the finished cushion a straight border (Fig. 6-3). Assemble a fabric-stuffing-fabric sandwich

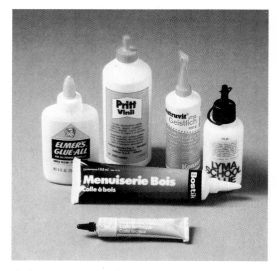

6-2. An international selection of glues: white glues (top); fabric glue (bottom).

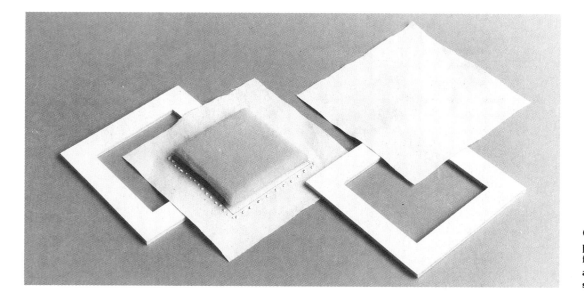

6-3. Upholstering a cushion: Note the soft polyurethane foam padding, two foamcore frames for obtaining a double-convex shape, and the glue dots placed just outside of the seam line.

and either clamp it between the foamcore frames or place it on the work surface, cover it with the single frame, and apply weights (Fig. 6-4). Allow ample drying time before removing the cushion from the frame (Fig. 6-5).

Trim off the extra fabric with a pair of sharp scissors (Fig. 6-6). Use a bit of diluted glue on a small brush to fix threads and touch up spots that may not have stuck together.

6-4. Upholstering a cushion: The frames are held together with hair clips while the glue is drying.

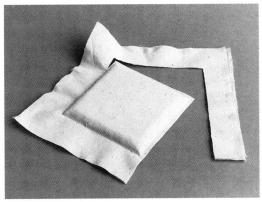

6-5 (left). Upholstering a cushion: The glued fabric looks as if it has been sewn.

6-6 (above). Upholstering a cushion: Trimming off the excess fabric after the glue has dried.

RUBBER

Rubber parts can often be represented with another material, such as paper. Examples of this can be found in Chapter 1, Special Effects. It is, however, sometimes appropriate to use real rubber for details, to give an appealing touch of realism to the model. This is particularly true for models made with symbolic materials such as paper and foam. A detail made with the true material not only adds realism to the model, but often produces an interesting contrast to the symbolic material.

We use real rubber in this manner only for 1:1 scale details—handles, chair arms, and other parts of a product the user will come in contact with. And we use only textured rubber because it looks the way people imagine rubber to be and therefore effectively communicates the concept of rubber. Smooth rubber can be convincingly represented by paper and therefore the additional effort of using real rubber is not justified.

MATERIALS AND SUPPLIES

Rubber—a few types of textured rubber, such as those with parallel lines, dots, and diamonds, are available at specialized dealers (Fig. 6-7). Rubber can rarely be found in colors other than black. Sometimes it is possible to find other textured materials, such as vinyl and polyurethane, in stores selling imitation leather and specialty fabrics. Synthetics look similar to rubber and are usually available in colors (Fig. 6-8).

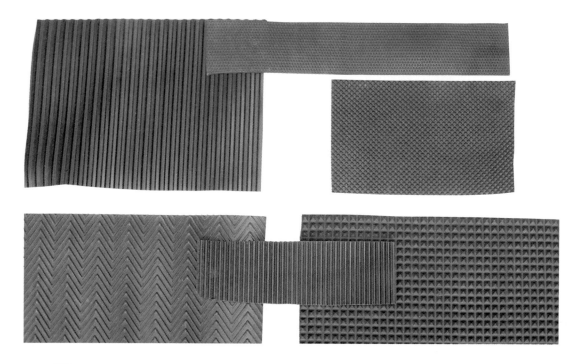

6-7. A selection of textured rubber.

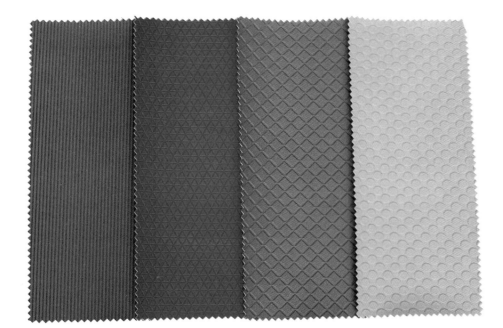

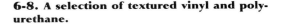
**6-8. A selection of textured vinyl and poly-
urethane.**

Tools—the same tools used for paper are adequate for working with rubber (see Chapter 1).

Adhesives—contact cement and cyanoacrylate are recommended for rubber. Because cyanoacrylate will not fill gaps, surfaces to be bonded must mate tightly. Do not use cyanoacrylate on large surfaces.

For vinyl and polyurethane, use contact cement.

Finishing supplies—trichloroethylene or other dry cleaning fluids; 120- to 200-grit abrasive paper; spray paint.

WORKING WITH RUBBER

When using real rubber in a model, do not leave the edge of the rubber exposed. Rubber is usually much thicker than paper and sometimes has a canvas backing; furthermore, cuts often lack precision. For these reasons an open edge makes a poor finish. Use a mat knife for straight cuts and scissors for round or complex shapes. Designing a border made out of the model's material (paper, foam, wood) around the rubber insert solves this.

Since real rubber is usually available only in black, it may be necessary to paint it. We do not suggest special rubber paints because they are hard to find, sold only in large cans, and available in a limited range of colors. Equally serious, being thick, they tend to cover up the rubber texture. The flexibility provided by rubber paint (it will not crack when the rubber surface is bent) rarely is needed in a model, which is static. For all these reasons, we strongly recommend using normal spray paint.

Prepare surfaces to be painted with a light sanding and thorough cleaning.

We have briefly mentioned the issue of realism in models. It should by now be clear that our view of realism does not mean building exact replicas of final products. Model-making should not be seen as a matter of pure realistic representation. On the contrary, one of the features of the design–process approach that we stress is that models should be *designed,* as the result of a creative process, not just made. This often involves researching ways to achieve realistic effects without necessarily reproducing exactly the material, shape, or details of the final product. Working with ready-made and found objects is one of the best time-saving ways to achieve a realistic look in a model.

For example, the wheel of a child's toy can serve as a knob for a radio or an air-conditioning unit with the simple addition of a paper cap of the color appropriate (Figs. 7-1, 7-2). The material (molded plastic or rubber) and the surface quality of a toy wheel provide the realistic effect usually found in a knob. The traditional alternative to this would be to use a lathe to turn a knob from a wooden dowel. In most cases the result of all that work would not be as convincing as the toy wheel because the toy is made of molded plastic just as the real knob is. Small but important details such as the flash line and textured surface provide that touch of realism. Another type of knob might be well represented by the cap from a tube of toothpaste or glue. These are just two of the almost unlimited possibilities.

The designer who uses imagination when looking at everyday objects will be well rewarded. Our world is so full of useful and useless products that we tend not to "see" them anymore. By seeing them in terms of form and color, not as specific objects, the designer will discover an endless source of ready-made material for model-making.

7-1. Toys can provide a rich supply of found objects.

7-2. The toy airplane's wheel has been transformed into a knob, with the addition of a paper cap.

COLLECTING AND ORGANIZING FOUND OBJECTS

Instead of looking around for ready-made objects when the need arrives, it is better to start a collection of interesting shapes with potentialities. Keep your eyes open!

Disposable products, vacuum-formed packaging, pen refills, caps, wheels, tubes, parts from old electric appliances and toys, Christmas decorations, beads, gaskets, plastic casings, and electric wire are just a few items worth collecting (Figs. 7-3, 7-4, 7-5, 7-6, 7-7).

These and other objects will be most useful if they are divided by form and shape in a series of containers. Such a well-ordered warehouse will save time when a particular shape is needed. The storage containers should be organized like a stock room, divided by shape and size, making it simple to locate a particular type of item, such as a button or tubular sheath, as the need arises.

Plastic boxes divided into compartments, such as those intended for buttons and other sewing notions or for nails, screws, bolts and other hardware are useful storage options. Small cardboard boxes, such as cigar or shoe boxes are other possibilities. A storage arrangement can be custom built. Before buying or building storage units be sure that they are open in a way that provides easy access and inspection. Label each container according to its contents.

7-3. Found objects: toy wheels.

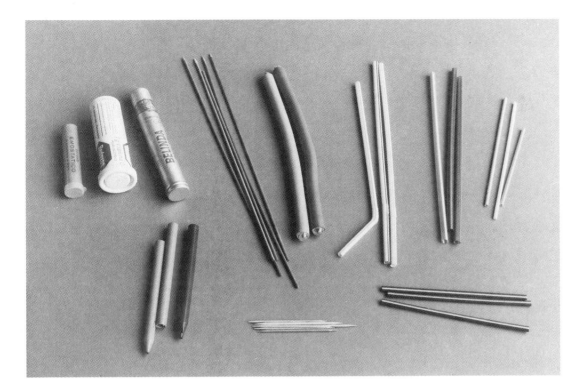

7-4. Found objects: sticks and tubes. Top row, left to right: pill and cigar cases, wooden skewers, soft rubber hair ties, drinking straws, plastic stirrers; bottom row, left to right: empty ballpoint pens, wooden toothpicks, plastic stirrers.

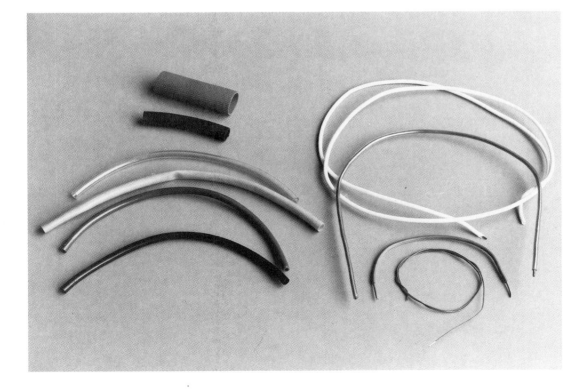

7-5. Found objects: vinyl tubes and electrical wiring.

7-6. Found objects: corrugated plastic tubes—toy parts and electrical wire sleeves.

7-7. Found objects: spherical forms— Christmas decorations, bubble packaging, and caps.

TOOLS AND SUPPLIES

The tools needed for working with found objects are the all-purpose ones mentioned throughout this book, the specifics varying with the primary material from which the model is made. Likewise, the adhesive used depends on the material the found object is made of and the material to which it is to be bonded. It is probable that most of the objects will be plastic, so we suggest keeping in stock the whole range of glues suggested in Chapter 5. Silicone sealant can be particularly handy because of its capacity to fill gaps. Keep in mind, however, that it is messy to work with; take care and use only in small amounts.

WORKING WITH FOUND OBJECTS

There is no single way to attach found objects to models; each situation has its own specific requirements, depending on the form and the materials in question. See assembling and gluing advice for specific materials in the chapters devoted to each. Many times it will be necessary to insert connecting elements into the model to hold the found object.

In general we do not suggest painting found objects; when possible, try to choose the piece not only for its form but also for its color.

One of the problems with painting found objects is that chemical incompatibilities may arise between the plastic from which the objects is made and the solvents in a given paint. Polystyrene and ABS will be melted by most solvents, for example. Polyethylene and polypropylene have surface properties that resist adherence, so many paints will peel off when dry.

Polystyrene and ABS may survive a very light coat of paint and, similarly, paint may not peel off polyethylene and polypropylene, but this cannot be absolutely guaranteed, due to the great variety of plastic materials and corresponding reactions.

It is worth repeating that the model should always follow the properties of the material chosen for its execution. In the case of found objects, this may mean rethinking the shape of the model to fit the form and color of the available found objects. Sometimes we make models based on the inspiration we get from a particular found object that we have in stock.

Our simplified approach often demands a lot of ingenuity and sometimes even requires sacrifices in terms of shape and image. We do believe, however, that reaching a design goal through minimized effort is an important advantage gained from this way of thinking. We also feel the found object approach reflects a commitment to invention that should be inherent in a designer's creative attitude.

8  GRAPHICS

There are many specialized books dealing with product graphics and they are full of technical data and instructions. We do not aim to provide information at this level, nor to substitute for them with a few words. Nonetheless, our quick and easy approach has applications in this area as well.

There are basically two reasons for adding graphics to a model. First, graphic ideas need to be represented just as product design ideas do. In our case the model is the physical support on which the graphics will be placed. Second, graphics add realism to the model. Well-proportioned graphics well placed on a model help convey the function of the product. Personalizing the model with the client's logo or trademark is an extra courtesy. Graphics alone cannot improve a poor design, but they can induce the client to be more open to innovative ideas, especially in a model that has the company's logo on it.

Two types of graphics are usually applied on industrial design models: instructions and the name of the product or manufacturer or both.

Although special equipment exists for making graphics and for applying lettering to models, we prefer to do without expensive and complex equipment.

INSTRUCTIONS

This type of graphics needs to be designed with great attention because it must clearly communicate how to operate the product. Often the manufacturer's technical staff will specify the text that must appear on the product; the designer's task is to properly arrange, space, and proportion the lettering or the symbols. At other times it is considered part of the general design job to develop and to graphically arrange directions for the user.

Instructions are either written in one or more languages or are symbolized. The second option is being used increasingly, especially in Europe, where translation into four or five languages might otherwise be required.

We use dry transfer lettering for both words and symbols. The use of transfer lettering is certainly obvious and standard in the case of words, but may not be as readily apparent in the case of symbols. Nonetheless, creative possibilities exist. Although the major manufacturers of dry transfer lettering (Letraset and others) produce symbols as well, most are specifically for technical architectural and engineering work. A few can also be used on product design models, but they are often hard to find and typically are available in black and only very rarely in white. Moreover, it may be necessary to buy a whole sheet just for one symbol.

For these reasons we have developed a way to do without ready-made transfer symbols. It requires seeing type as pure form. Most frequently we use sans serif letters, numerals, and a few very simple graphic elements, such as dots, squares, and lines, assembling them to create new or represent existing symbols for the various functions (Figs. 8-1 through 8-20). A few sans serif types are available in six colors. If the graphics are black against a white background or vice versa, enlargement or reduction by photocopying is possible.

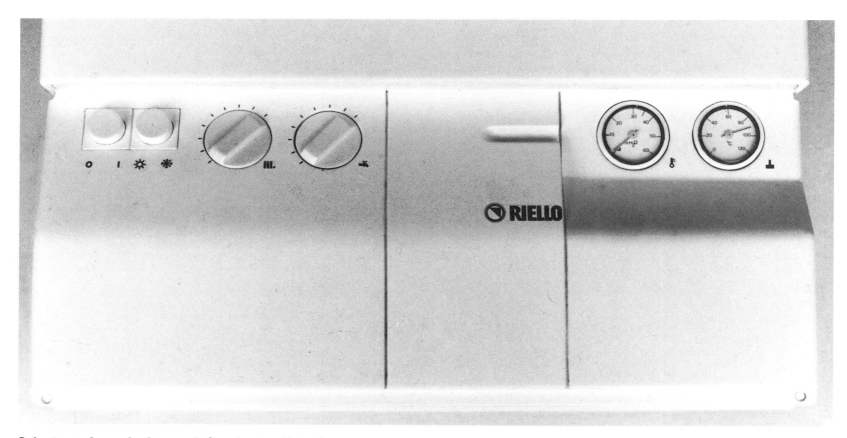

8-1. Control panel of a gas boiler heater. Note the company's logo (center) and the symbols (left to right): on/off; summer/winter selector switch; heater thermostat; boiler thermostat; temperature and pressure gauges.

8-2, 8-3. Using dry transfer to make the sun symbol (summer selector switch) with the lowercase letter *o* and dashes.

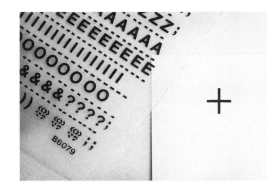

8-4, 8-5, 8-6. Using dry transfer to make the snowflake symbol (winter selector switch) with four capital letters *I* and quotation marks.

8-7, 8-8. Using dry transfer to make the radiator symbol (heater thermostat) with three lowercase letters *i* without dots and one *i*'s dot.

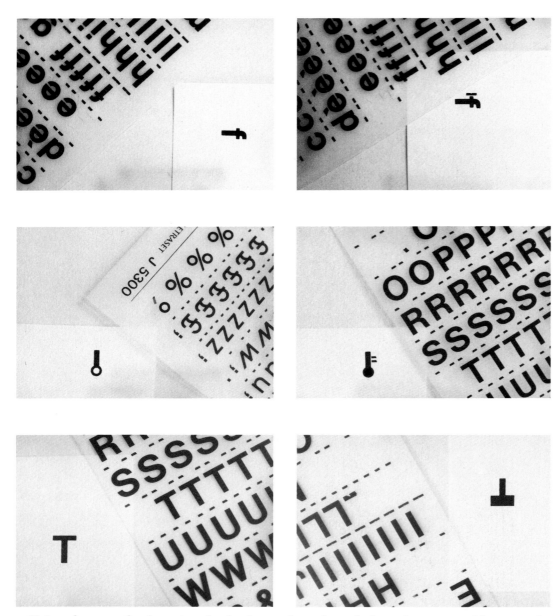

8-9, 8-10. Using dry transfer to make the hot-water faucet symbol (boiler thermostat) with the lowercase letter *f* and two dashes.

8-11, 8-12. Using dry transfer to make the temperature gauge with the lowercase letter *i* without its dot, two dashes, and the zero from the percent sign. The zero is touched up by darkening the center with black ink.

8-13, 8-14. Using dry transfer to make the pressure gauge with the capital letters *T* and *I.*

Using dry transfer lettering for both words and symbols makes it possible to apply graphics directly to the surface of the model (except foam). A light coat of matte fixative will cover all traces of the transfer's adhesive.

In cases when it is awkward to center and properly space lettering and symbols directly on the model, we suggest applying them to a sheet of paper of the same color as the model. Cut around the symbol, leaving as little paper as possible, then position and glue the bit of paper onto the surface of the model. Use a pair of tweezers and either white glue or rubber cement to do the job. If very little blank space is left around the graphic, it will hardly be noticeable, even if the colors of the two surfaces do not match perfectly.

8-15. The symbols cut out with as little white paper as possible left around them. Note that the model (Figure 8-1) is also white.

8-16. Removable control panel of an air-conditioning unit. Note the company logo (top) and the symbols (top to bottom): on/off, fault, fan, and thermostat.

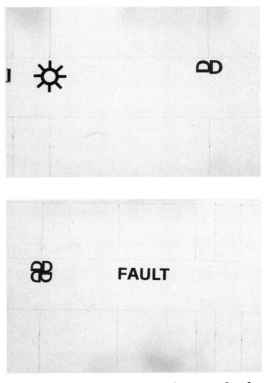

8-17, 8-18. Using dry transfer to make the fan symbol with four capital letters *D*.

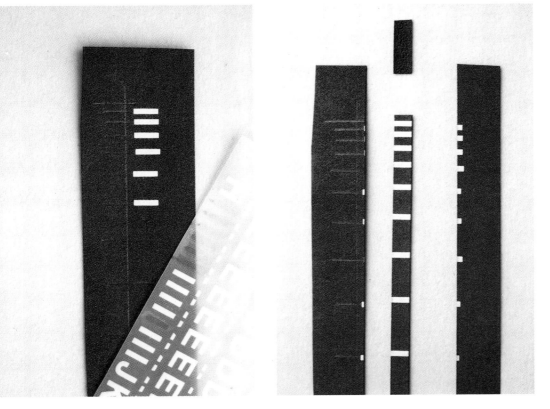

8-19, 8-20. Using dry transfer to make the thermostat's scale with six white capital *I*'s on black paper. Trimming down the excess black paper not only gives the graduated look of a thermometer but also eases alignment of the marks.

LOGOS

If the name of the product is not a logotype the procedure is the same as described above. If it is, obtain a brochure, magazine advertisement, letterhead, or other printed material from the client that includes a reproduction of the logotype you are looking for (Figs. 8-21, 8-22). If the size is not the right, have it reduced or enlarged as a photocopy. If color is required, you may either order a color photocopy or use colored pencil to match the color of the model.

Position and glue finished artwork onto the model as described.

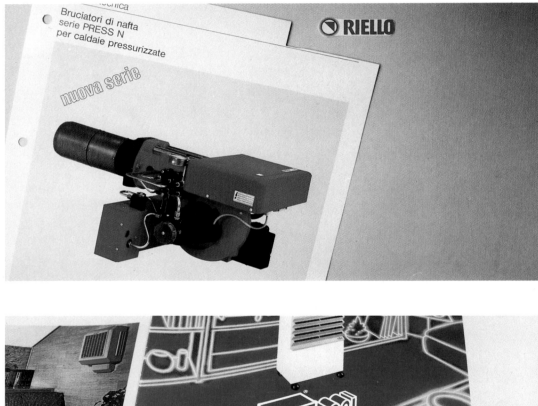

8-21. A company logo cut from a product brochure. It is glued in place in the model pictured in Figure 8-1.

8-22. A company logo white on black cut from a product brochure. It is glued in place on the model pictured in Figure 8-16.

Emblems with the name of the product or company can easily be made by cutting out the logo from a brochure or other printed material. In this case, cut out the logo in a regular geometric shape, which will be the shape of the emblem. Glue it onto a slightly larger piece of black three-ply paper to create a black contour around the logo. The procedure and effect are similar to those described for making LEDs (see Chapter 1, Special Effects).

The emblem can be enriched by interposing a piece of adhesive foil or metallic paper (chrome, gold, copper) between the logo and the piece of black paper. The emblem will then have two contours, one in metal and one in black (Figs. 8-23, 8-24).

8-23, 8-24. Making an emblem: A three-dimensional effect is achieved by placing the logo on top of a piece of black paper, which is in turn mounted on chrome foil.

For the designer, photography is the only practical way to preserve a record of a model. Whether a model is made for checking a form, for presentation to a client, or as a step in the design process it rarely is made to last. In most cases the model either will be given to the client (who pays for it), modified, or destroyed. Photographing all models is important not only as a record of the work made but also as a reference for any additional work that might be necessary. We regret not having photographed all of our models. Many of them are missing in this book; they are lost forever!

Our simplified approach to model-making has its corollary in the photographing of models. Within limits our results can often reach the standards of professional photography, if a few basic rules are followed.

Work only with natural light and with the conditions of light intensity and color specified later in the text.

Do not use this approach to photograph very large objects, such as desks, tables, bookshelves. Such large models should be professionally photographed. If the photo is for your own record, however, and will not be used for presentation or publication, our method will produce acceptable results.

Keep the set as simple as possible. Fancy ideas usually require professional skills and equipment to produce good photographs.

EQUIPMENT

Camera—a 35mm single-lens reflex camera with an automatic shutter release (timer) and electronic shutter control for long time exposures is the only kind suitable for this kind of work. A cheap camera with a viewfinder and noninterchangeable lens will not permit the precision required. Professional cameras, such as large-format single-lens reflexes, require a lot of equipment and a professional studio. Precision in positioning the camera, focusing, and exposure as well as sophisticated control of lighting are necessary, all of which are inconsistent with our simplified approach.

Lens—a short telephoto lens (90, 105, or 135mm). Most of the photos should be shot with the telephoto lens, because it reduces the optical deformations of objects viewed in perspective, in effect adjusting three-dimensional objects to two-dimensionality. In general, use a normal lens (50mm) only when the subject is too big or too close to the camera for a telephoto lens.

Tripod—a heavy, precision-built tripod with a fully articulated head is absolutely necessary. A cheap, lightweight tripod will not allow correct positioning of the camera and will shake in long time exposures. Never shoot holding the camera in your hands; besides shaking the camera, you will invariably end up with the subject not in the position you wanted.

Film—at present, color slide film is the least expensive and most flexible way to take photographs; it is the best medium for obtaining both good quality color transparencies and color prints. In the future some new kind of film may appear and solve some of the many problems of photography. We prefer to use 100 ASA; faster film is too grainy for photographing models.

Background—a few sheets of colored three-ply paper (minimum size: 30 by 40 inches/750 × 1000mm) should be kept in stock for photographing small items, such as scale models. For larger subjects use seamless background paper, available at art supply and photo shops in a wide range of colors and various widths. We suggest buying rolls no wider than 60 inches (1500mm); wider paper is difficult to handle and easily spoiled.

Although it may be fun to use colored backgrounds, we almost always recommend a gray background; it will give your photos a serious professional look and will reduce the necessity to reshoot because of color problems. (Remember: Keep it simple.)

Miscellaneous—a couple of 30- by 40-inch (750 × 1000mm) white foamcore sheets or Styrofoam panels for controlling natural light; drafting tape for fixing in position the background and the foamcore sheets.

LIGHT

Light is the most complex and probably the most important aspect of our photography method. We mentioned that we use only natural light; the trick is in controlling this light source and accepting its limits.

A window is, from the dimensional point of view, our light module; the larger the window, the better. A thin white curtain will help diffuse the light and it is absolutely necessary if the window has many panes. It is important to take into consideration that curtains and heavy sashes absorb light; therefore, when they are unavoidable, more natural light is needed.

If the window receives direct sunlight, do not shoot at that time of day; wait until the light becomes indirect. Avoid early morning hours with intense blue sky (blue will dominate the photograph) and dark days (not enough light will hit the subject).

MAKING THE PHOTOGRAPH

SETTING UP

Assuming now that you have the right equipment and light, the first thing to do is to set the background. Place a table against a wall to either side of the window. Tape the sheet of three-ply paper or roll of seamless paper with drafting tape, so that part of it hangs vertically against the wall and part lies horizontally on the table, a soft curve linking the two surfaces. The amount of paper against the wall is determined by the height of the model to be photographed; clearly the height of the background must exceed that of the subject.

Mount the camera on the tripod. If possible, keep the film plane parallel to the vertical surface of the background. The height of the camera is determined by the angle at which you want to picture the subject (from above, from the same level, from below).

POSITIONING AND LIGHTING THE MODEL

Decide how you want to see the model in the photograph. We do not recommend photographing the model at too narrow an angle from above or from aside; all the parallel lines in the picture will be slanted and convergent. The telephoto lens reduces but cannot eliminate this effect.

After roughly positioning the subject against the background, it is extremely important to control the light and the shades. The dark and recessed areas of the model should receive the maximum light, otherwise they will be black in the picture. Rotate the model consequently until its darkest part is properly lighted.

Sometimes an area receives too much light. The details will appear overexposed in the picture. When rotating the model, be aware of areas that are too bright.

If not enough light hits the darkest areas, experiment with positioning one or two sheets of white foamcore or Styrofoam to reflect the natural light against the shady area of the model.

Correct control of lights and shade is particularly important when the model is black or dark gray. Poor light control will produce a photo of a black spot instead of the model (Fig. 9-1).

EXPOSURE

In general we suggest overexposing one half stop, that is, by setting the light meter on 75 ASA instead of 100 if you are using 100 ASA film. This will help to make all the details clearly visible. If the model is white or any other very bright color, do not overexpose. If the model is black, however, overexpose by one stop (set at 50 ASA instead of 100).

Small lens openings (f:16 or f:22) give the depth of field required to get the whole model in focus. Since only a modest amount of natural light is available under the conditions described, exposure times must be long. This is why an electronic shutter control is handy. Avoid speeds from one-quarter to one second; the double movement of the shutter may result in a shaken picture, especially if the tripod is less than professional quality. Two- to fifteen-second exposures are recommended. Exposures

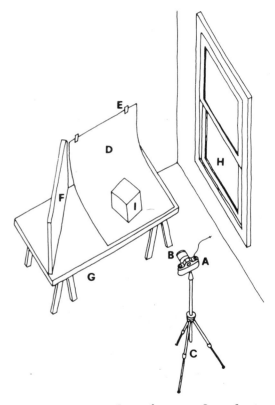

9-1. The set and equipment for photographing a model.

A. **35mm single-lens reflex camera**
B. **Telephoto lens (90–135mm)**
C. **Tripod**
D. **Three-ply paper background**
E. **Drafting tape**
F. **Foamcore or Styrofoam panel**
G. **Table**
H. **Window**
I. **Model**

over thirty seconds may require adjusting the light meter down another half stop or more. Rather than such long exposures, however, we recommend using a lower f-stop to admit more light.

Bracket exposures by taking at least three shots of any subject, one with what you think is the right exposure, one slightly overexposed, and the third slightly under-exposed. In this way you will almost always be sure to have one well-exposed picture with all the details of the model clearly visible.

10 ◻◻◻ PROTECTING AND TRANSPORTING MODELS

Almost all of the materials discussed in this book are very delicate. Even sturdy materials such as metal and plastic are often assembled with glues that make even more delicate models than those built out of paper or foam. All models can very easily be spoiled, and even destroyed, during transport and in long-term storage. Models need to be protected against jostling, shaking, dust, humidity, air, and sunlight.

The less a model is exposed to light and air, the longer it will last. Air oxidizes many glues; humidity warps paper and wood; light yellows white paint and paper and pales bright colors; dust fills in the pores of expanded resins.

During transport a model can easily be damaged: Glue joints may not be as strong as the materials they bond together; paper models may be crushed under even minimal pressure; foam and balsa wood, or parts, may break.

The best way to protect against damage is to pack the model in a suitably sturdy container. Properly designed, such a container also solves the problem of presentation to the client. Opening a nice box with a small model hidden in it is a "ceremony" that draws attention to the model and interest to the design it represents.

Ideally, you should design and build a specific container for every model. If the model is very large or if there is no time to build a box, at least wrap up the model with a few sheets of tissue paper. Never leave work unprotected.

Foamcore, chipboard, corrugated board, and cardboard are suitable for most types of boxes, and for some larger ones. A large or very delicate model or any model that is to be shipped should be protected in a wooden crate.

Building a box is like building a paper model, so the construction methods for foamcore and corrugated board, outlined in Chapter 1, apply. Remember that a box has to be strong; reinforce all joints on the inside with extra curbs of glue and stick straight pins into the foamcore or corrugated board corners.

When designing the box be sure to provide it with partitions and inside ribbings; they can be made out of foamcore, corrugated board, or hard foams. They will keep the model tightly in position and protect it against damage during transport. Partitions are also useful for separating any additional or interchangeable parts of the model. Do not use soft foam for making the partitions because they will allow the model to move inside the box, which may lead to damage. If the model is made of different materials with different weights, it is particularly crucial to position it in such a way that the heavy parts cannot move or else these heavier parts will act as a hammer on the lighter ones.

Large or bulky boxes need a handle for easy transportation. Make a handle by laminating together three or four strips of three-ply paper (see Chapter 1, Lamination) or use a plastic handle taken from a strong shopping bag. Another good solution is one of a large selection of plastic and metal handles designed for cabinet doors and drawers available at reasonable prices at hardware and home improvement stores. These handles normally have holes to fix them by means of screws to the foamcore or corrugated board box. Insert a large washer between the head of the screw and the surface of the board to avoid any deformation or laceration of the box.

Finally, having made a suitable container always keep the model in it!

Although each model will dictate the form of the container to be built for it, we offer some ideas based on containers we have made (Figs. 10-1 through 10-14). Each was designed with both protection and presentation in mind.

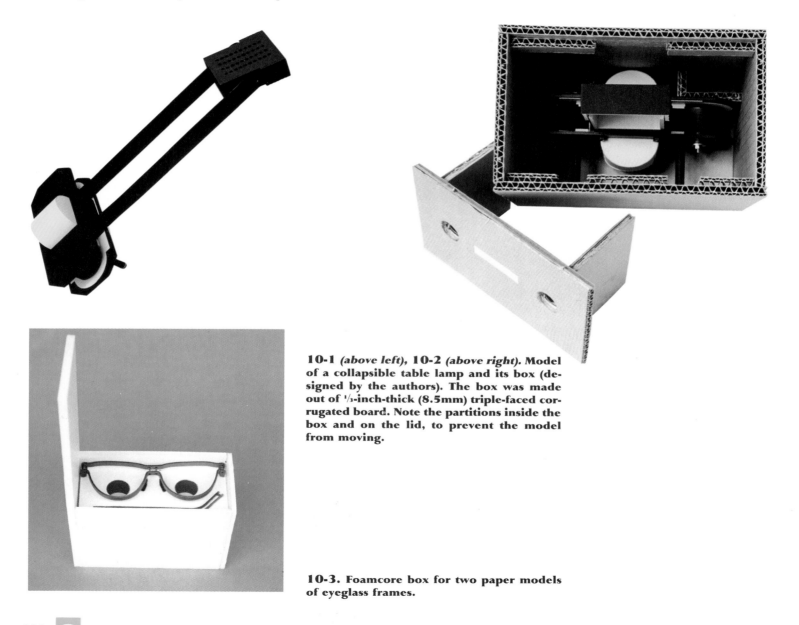

10-1 *(above left)*, **10-2** *(above right)*. Model of a collapsible table lamp and its box (designed by the authors). The box was made out of ¹⁄₃-inch-thick (8.5mm) triple-faced corrugated board. Note the partitions inside the box and on the lid, to prevent the model from moving.

10-3. Foamcore box for two paper models of eyeglass frames.

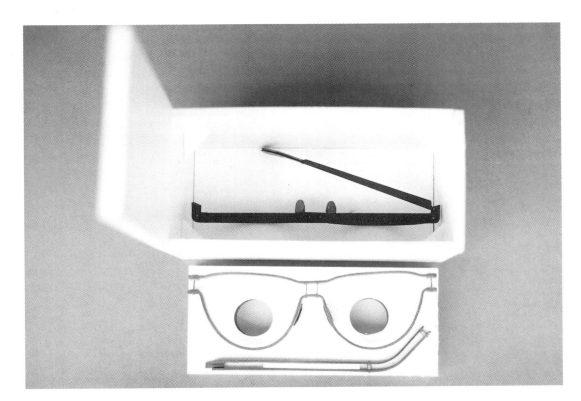

10-4. Foamcore box shown in Figure 10-3. Note that the internal partition is removable and functions as a tray for one of the two models.

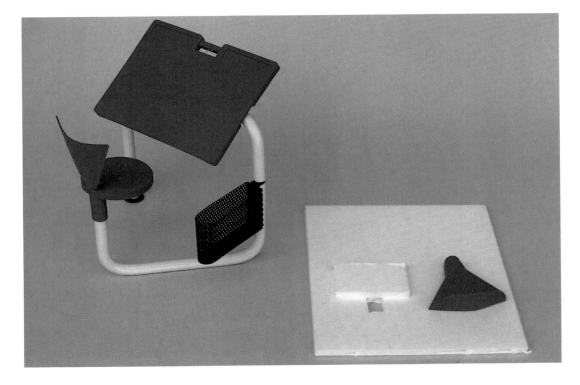

10-5. A paper and plastic 1:4 scale model of a child's desk and chair unit with perforated metal book container (designed by the authors). Note the interchangeable saddle-like seat on the foamcore tray.

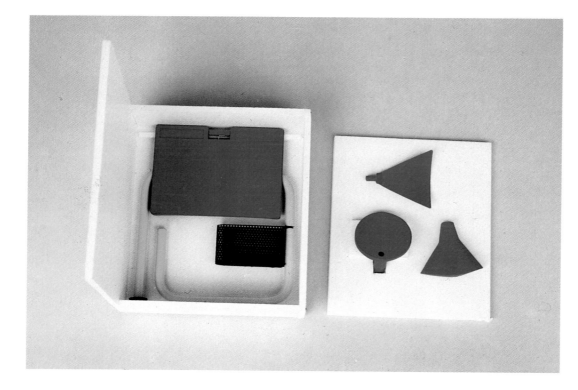

10-6 *(left).* Foamcore box for carrying the desk unit seen in Figure 10-5. The foamcore tray carries the backrest and the two seat options shown to the client.

10-7 *(above).* Foamcore box for carrying a 1:10 scale model of a baby's bath trolley (designed by the authors). The box is just big enough for the model to slide inside. Once the lid is closed the model cannot move.

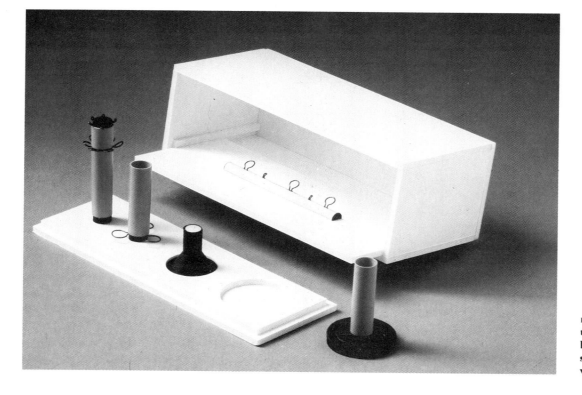

10-8. Foamcore box for carrying a 1:6 scale model of a collapsible coat tree (designed by the authors). The double layer foamcore base holds the disassembled elements. The sliding tray inside the box's top holds the wall version of the coat rack.

10-9. A paper and plastic 1:4 scale model of a collapsible chair (designed by the authors).

10-10. The disassembled chair slides into a chipboard box. The handle was made by laminating four strips of black three-ply paper.

10-11. A paper, wood, and metal system model (scale 1:4) of a chair (designed by the authors). The disassembled parts in the foreground can be interchanged with the elements of the standing chair to create many different design options.

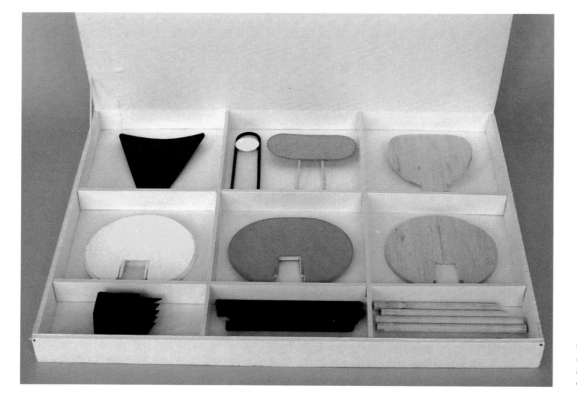

10-12. Foamcore box containing all the design options of the chair. Note that the parts are loose in the compartments of the box and, as a consequence, a few were damaged during transportation to the client.

MATERIALS AND TECHNIQUES

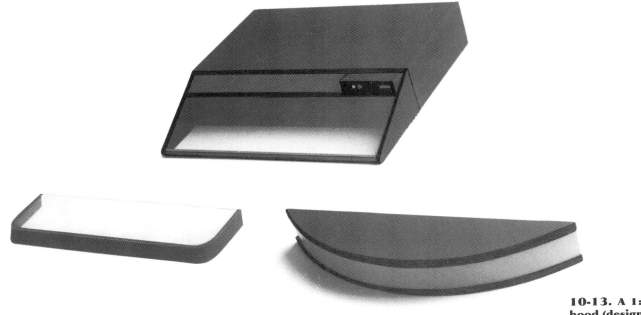

10-13. A 1:3 scale paper model of a stove hood (designed by the authors) with two design options for the front side.

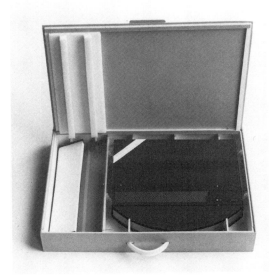

10-14. Chipboard case reinforced with foamcore for carrying the stove hood model. Note the Styrofoam partitions on the left; the plastic handle taken from a shopping bag.

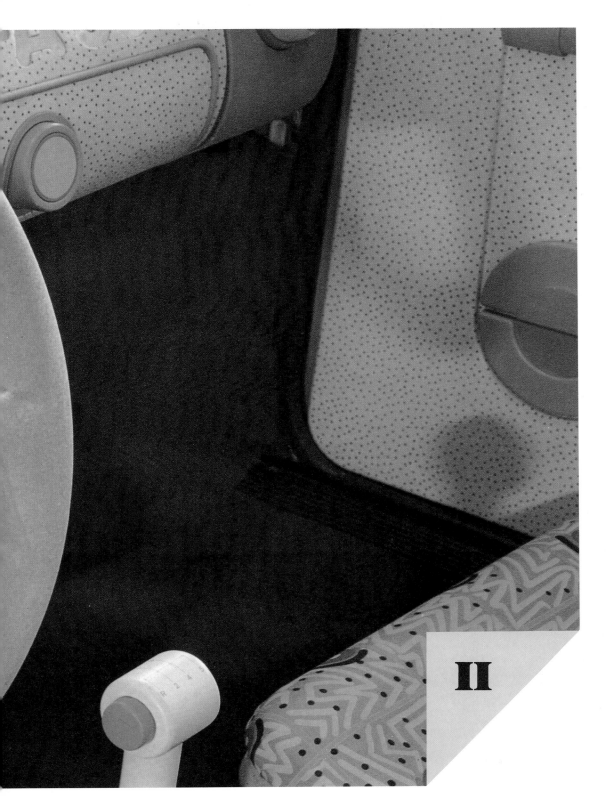

II

EXAMPLES

In this part of the book we present the models and the projects built in our office or in the school where we have taught, following the techniques and using the materials described in Part I. Since Part I is divided into chapters according to materials, we have divided Part II the same way. This scheme will help the reader find examples that correspond to the materials discussed in Part I.

When more than one material has been used in building a model, we have categorized it according to the most significant material used; this is often the material that contributes the most to portraying a concept. A few times we have listed a model under a certain material because parts of the model, sometimes just details, exemplify the use of that particular material. In all cases we placed the examples where they would best show the use of a given material and technique. Therefore we invite the reader to try to understand why some models are grouped where one would not expect to see them.

All of the models shown here clearly express our model-making philosophy. The majority were made in our office; a few were made by our students.

Many were not built by highly skilled people.

In common with most design offices, ours offers part-time jobs to design students. Some of them are good model-makers, the majority are not. A similar generalization can be made for the school projects, which are open to all students, skilled and unskilled. The same can also be said of the authors: Paolo Orlandini is a good model-maker, Roberto Lucci is not. All the same, this book is full of acceptable-quality presentation models. We offer this as conclusive evidence that our model-making methods can be followed with success by almost everyone. The rules explained in Part I are simple; following them carefully virtually guarantees success.

As we have said before, we regret not being able to show all of our models. Quite a few of the early ones (built from 1968 to 1980) were destroyed without having been photographed. What we regret most is not having photographed many of the quick models we made during the early phases of the design process. They would have been helpful in better demonstrating our design process approach, which uses model-making as a way to sketching in three dimensions. We are convinced that the best way to check design ideas is to actually see them three-dimensionally. In our opinion, no two-dimensional rendering can serve the designer as well as a three-dimensional form, which offers certainties on what to do and how to proceed.

▲ 11-1

▲ 11-2

FIGURES 11-1, 11-2, 11-3

Plastic stacking tables, "Rondo" and "Madison"; designed by the authors, 1987; manufactured by Grazioli-Grand Soleil, Mosio (Mantua), Italy.

The real product is shown in Figure 11-1; Figures 11-2 and 11-3 show the 1:4 scale models of the tables, which were made with white three-ply construction paper. Embossed top surface of the round table was achieved by gluing together two sheets of three-ply paper (see Special Effects, Chapter 1). The textured surface on the square table was obtained from a sheet of self-adhesive tone (Letratone).

This project includes the chair shown in Figures 11-4 to 11-9. It aimed at producing one-piece, all-plastic furniture to be sold at very low prices. The products are molded in polypropylene. Because of the resin's relatively low stiffness, these tables and chairs had to be designed with a structural shape—the most critical parts (legs and legs-to-plane connection) had to

be shaped in a way that maximizes the stiffness of a thin and otherwise flexible material.

Paper was a great help, not only for making attractive models in a short time, but in guiding us to design a structural shape. The accordionlike section of the legs is a typical way to stiffen paper and, by analogy, thin plastic.

The stacking feature and the goal of a low price, requiring constant thickness and a minimum of material, respectively, were other factors that made paper an ideal material for solving the project's difficulty.

We must acknowledge that the design of these pieces (the chair in particular) is not exciting. The manufacturer had to compete in a crowded market, and the investment for the molds was quite heavy; therefore, the design was planned to entail as little risk (and innovation) as possible.

11-3 ▶

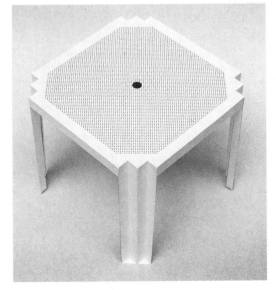

FIGURE 11-4

11-4

Plastic stacking chair, "Diva"; designed by the authors, 1987; manufactured by Grazioli-Grand Soleil, Mosio (Mantua), Italy; 1:4 scale model.

The concept behind this design has been described in Figures 11-1, 11-2 and 11-3. This scale model was made for the first presentation to the client. The textured surface of the seat has been shown and described in Special Effects, Chapter 1, Figure 1-59.

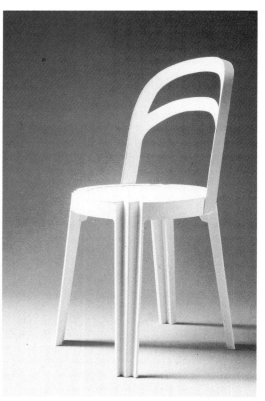

11-5

11-6

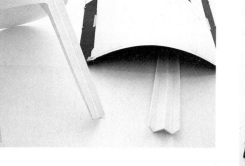

11-7

FIGURES 11-5, 11-6, 11-7

Plastic stacking chair, "Diva"; full-size model and construction details.

This model was built to enable the client's marketing and technical staff to better evaluate the new design. A new shape for the legs was introduced as an improvement over the first model.

The legs and the seat (Fig. 11-6) were made of foamcore and then covered with white two-ply paper. The backrest (Fig. 11-7) was made of laminated white three-ply paper. Note the piece of Masonite screwed onto a board to form a bow. We used it as a mold for laminating the chair's backrest.

FIGURE 11-8

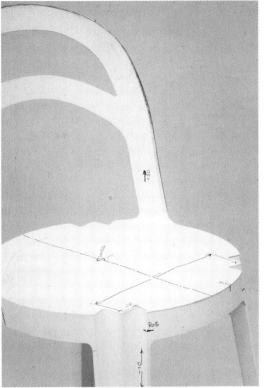

11-8

Plastic stacking chair, "Diva." Instead of a technical drawing, the paper 1:1 scale model seen in Figure 11-5 was given to a professional model-maker for building a full-size wooden model. Note the marks on the paper model used for specifying and correcting the details of the design.

11-10

FIGURE 11-10

11-9

FIGURE 11-9

Plastic stacking chair, "Diva"; full-size wooden model.

This final model was built to get a more precise evaluation of the details that could not be seen in the paper model (the spherical forms) and for the construction of the molds. A precision wooden or epoxy model (master) is often employed for reproducing the shape of the model in the mold.

Note the different shape of the backrest introduced to increase its resistance and to satisfy a request of the marketing department.

Plastic stacking chair and armchair; designed by the authors, 1986; project; full-size paper model.

This model was made of foamcore covered by white two-ply paper. It was an attempt to create a one-piece, all-plastic chair characterized by an unconventional design for this category of products. The grid seat and backrest would have provided a strong structure to the chair and good ventilation for the seated person, a much-appreciated feature for a garden chair that would be used mainly in the summer.

However, the highly competitive market of plastic outdoor chairs discouraged further development of this design. This chair would have been more expensive (more material, more costly molds) than most competing products.

FIGURE **11-11**

11-11

Stacking chair, "K"; designed by the authors, 1974; manufactured by Velca, Legnano (Milan), Italy.

All the structural parts of this seating system are made from deep-drawn sheet metal. A large number of different chairs can be produced from a basic set of elements. The complexity of the design is derived from the number of functions that must be performed by the system's common elements and also from the limitations of the deep-drawing technology. Therefore, all of the chair's basic elements had to be thoroughly designed.

FIGURE **11-12**

Stacking chair, "K." This 1:5 scale model was one of the first models made while designing the "K" seating system (1969).

The paper (black and colored three-ply) was shaped in the same way sheet metal would have been in the real product. Many changes had to be made during the design process, most of them to meet the requirements of sheet metal deep-drawing technology.

11-12

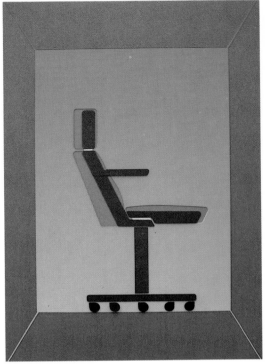

11-13

11-14

11-15

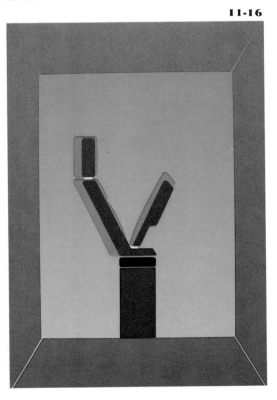

11-16

FIGURES 11-13, 11-14, 11-15, 11-16

Seating System; designed by the authors, 1984; project; two-dimensional modular 1:4 scale model.

This simple two-dimensional model was made to show the client the concept of an ergonomic seating system for office and public spaces. A basic set of elements was cut out of colored three-ply paper and positioned without glue on a sheet of color shade paper used as a background. The chair's parts were rearranged in each photograph.

The model did not really exist; it was assembled several times with different configurations, but only to be photographed. This method of making models is a good time-saver and can be applied to the design of many product systems.

FIGURES 11-17, 11-18

11-17

Stacking chair, "City"; designed by the authors, 1982; manufactured by Lamm, San Secondo Parmense (Parma), Italy.

A plastic (seat) and metal (legs) chair in which these two elements are joined together to form a structure in the simplest possible way. The legs are cut from a rectangular tube and plugged into four rectangular housings in the molded ribbing under the seat. No tools or fasteners are needed to mount the chair, which is delivered unassembled.

The chair received an honorable mention by the Institute of Business Designers (IBD) and a commendation by the Resources Council Product Design Awards Program (ROSCOE), 1982.

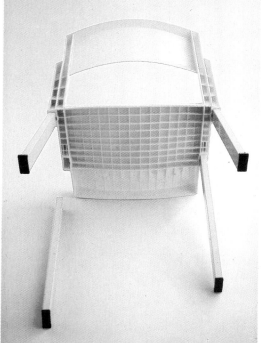

11-18

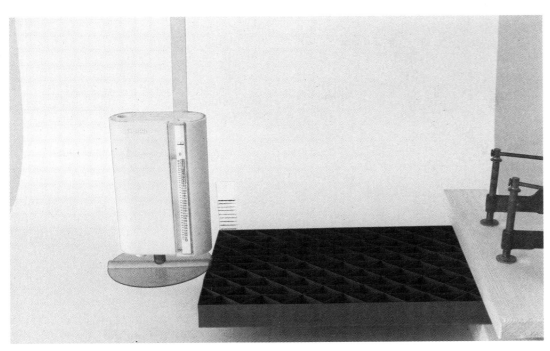

11-19

Stacking chair, "City"; structural tests.

Simple three-ply paper models were used to check the form of the plastic ribbing. A force was applied, and measured with a postal scale, to determine the resistance to deformation of the model's structure.

We eventually opted for a square module (not shown), which allowed for more elasticity in the chair's structure, thus reducing the possibility of breakage.

11-20

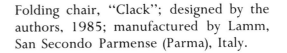

Folding chair, "Clack"; designed by the authors, 1985; manufactured by Lamm, San Secondo Parmense (Parma), Italy.

The interesting feature of this folding chair is its compactness: when folded, the chair is nearly half the size of most common folding chairs.

The seat and backrest are made of thermoplastic resin, the frame is steel tubing. (Photo 11-21: Paolo Gepri)

11-22

◀ **11-21**

FIGURE **11-23**

11-23

Folding chair, "Clack."

The first full-size model was built following a design concept different from that of the production: The seat and the backrest were made entirely out of plastic and were connected by a hinge. The backrest folded onto the seat, as in the real product, but the lack of a metal structure required a plastic structure that was too heavy and too expensive. We decided, therefore, to reduce the size of the plastic backrest and to introduce a metal frame.

In the model, the seat and the backrest were made of laminated black three-ply paper and were fixed onto two U-shaped tube legs supplied by the client. The model could be folded like the real chair.

FIGURE 11-24

Stacking chair; designed by the authors, 1987; project.

A very simple design for a low-priced chair. In this 1:1 scale model the metal frame, including the legs, was made out of an oval steel tube supplied by the client.

The seat and the backrest were constructed from foamcore, bent and covered on both sides with colored three-ply paper. The supports of the arms and of the backrest were made from two sheets of foamcore laminated together and covered with black three-ply paper.

11-24

11-25

EXAMPLES

Chair, "Varia"; designed by the authors, 1986; manufactured by Lamm, San Secondo Parmense (Parma), Italy.

An ergonomic office chair with a new one-spring, multi-hinged tilting mechanism. Another interesting design feature is the thin plastic "membranelike" seat surface, which fits the shape of the seated person. This seat offers a comfort similar to that of an upholstered chair, even in the economical nonupholstered versions. (Photos: Paolo Gepri)

11-26

FIGURE 11-27

Chair, "Varia."

A full-size model was built utilizing an existing star base and a tubular frame supplied by the manufacturer. The seat and the backrest are equal in form and therefore in the real product they are made from the same mold. In the model they were made out of white three-ply paper. The arms were built out of foam-core covered on both sides with white two-ply paper. The accordion effect on the seat and backrest was made to imitate the textured surface of the real product.

11-27

FIGURE 11-28

Ergonomic chair, "Movia"; designed by the authors, 1985; manufactured by Fantoni, Osoppo (Udine), Italy.

This chair has a self-adjusting mechanism for seat and backrest that gives a constant support to the spine, even in relaxed sitting postures. The mechanism permits a sliding movement of the seat and backrest, as well as a tilting movement of the backrest.

The seat, backrest, and other components of the mechanism are made of thermoplastic resin; the legs are metal.

11-28

FIGURE 11-29

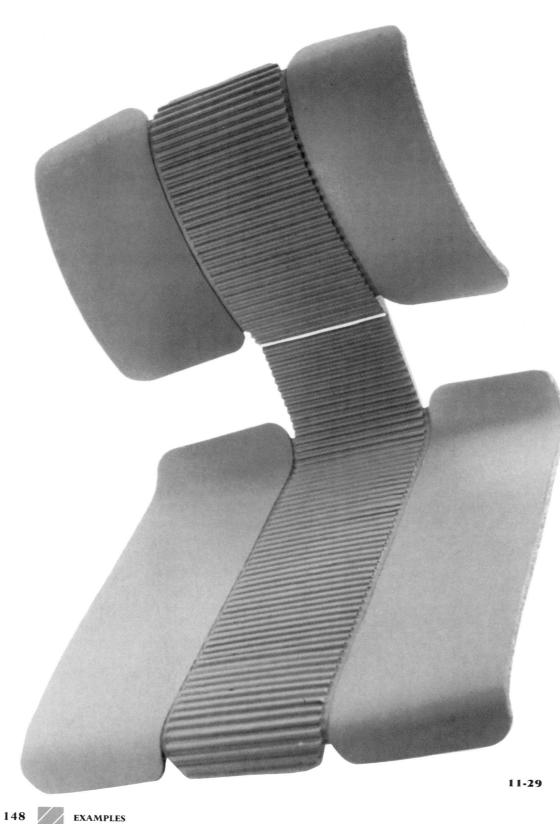

Ergonomic chair, "Movia"; full-size model of seat and backrest.

This model was made only to check the aesthetics; it was not a functional model. It was built with foamcore and single-faced corrugated paper (see also Fig. 1-60), over a rigid polyurethane foam support. The foamcore was curved and laminated with two-ply paper. The whole model was then painted with many thin coats of paint.

11-29

11-30

FIGURE **11-30**

Ergonomic chair, "Movia"; functional model of the self-adjusting mechanism.

While making the model in Figure 11-29 we also made this foamcore and three-ply paper model in order to see and demonstrate the chair's mechanism.

The backrest (left) was attached to a sled by means of a hinge that could slide up and down in the seat support (center). A sliding seat (right) was connected to the backrest by a flexible flap (upper right).

FIGURE 11-31

11-31

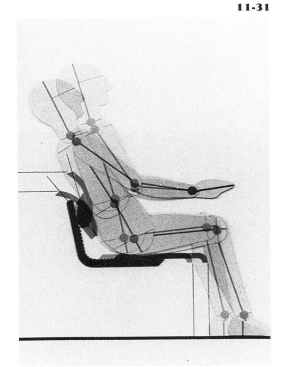

Ergonomic chair, "Movia"; two-dimensional model showing the movement of the seat and backrest.

This silhouette model, made with colored three-ply paper, was not glued but simply placed over a foamcore board. It was assembled in different positions and then photographed with a multiple exposure (see also Figs. 11-13 to 11-16).

FIGURE 11-32

11-32

Modular sofa; designed by the authors, 1970; project.

The idea was to produce a rigid polyurethane base that could be fitted with different tops to form sofas, ottomans, and tables.

The 1:5 scale model was made with glossy three-ply paper (base) and Canson Mi-Teintes colored one-ply paper (upholstery).

FIGURES 11-33, 11-34

11-33

11-34

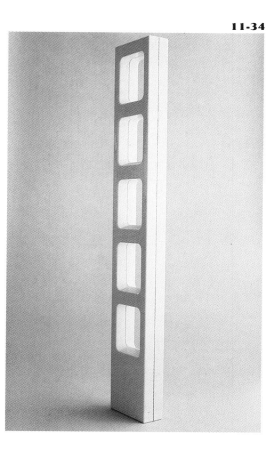

Household ladder, "Scaleo"; designed by the authors, 1973; manufactured by Velca, Legnano (Milan), Italy.

We designed this compact folding ladder with the purpose of giving a design dignity to an object that has traditionally received scarce attention from industrial designers. Ladders, in general, are heavy, awkward dust-catchers. As a consequence they are kept hidden and people tend to use a more accessible chair or table.

From the technical viewpoint the structure of this ladder is quite sophisticated: two ABS halves are reinforced by a light alloy structure glued to the ABS; the hinges include the locking device.

"Scaleo" is in the design collection of the Museum of Modern Art, New York.

11-35

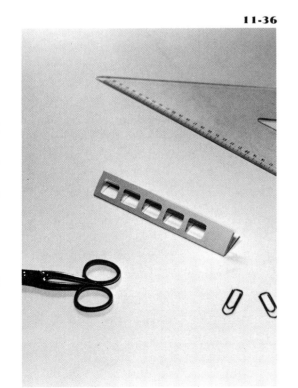

11-36

Household ladder, "Scaleo."

This elementary, three-ply paper 1:10 scale model represents one of the early design stages. It was the simple materialization of the basic design concept. The concept clearly derived from the very common action of folding a piece of paper, a further demonstration of how the properties of paper often produce design ideas.

Child's chalkboard; designed by the authors, 1986; project; 1:4 scale model.

Foamcore covered with colored three-ply paper; piano wire support. These photographs show how a typical paper model is made. Foamcore is employed for its structural properties and is covered with colored paper to obtain a finished look.

11-37

11-38

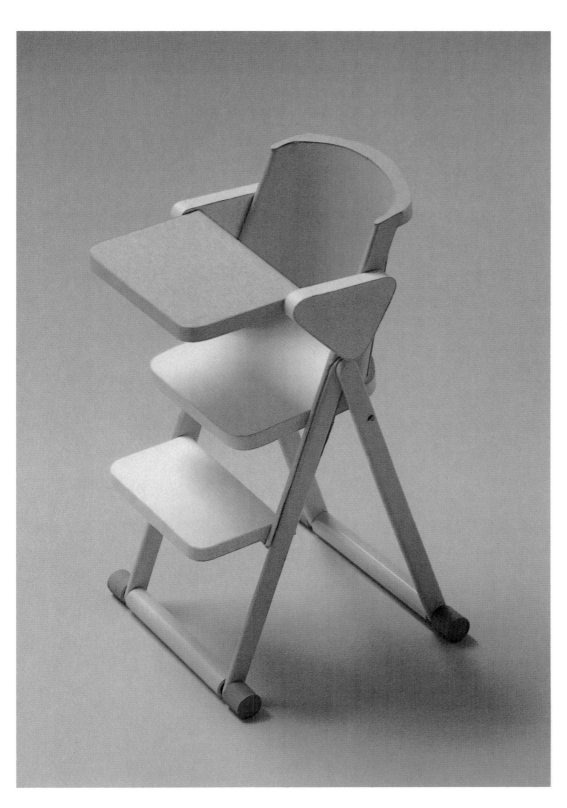

FIGURES 11-39, 11-40, 11-41

High chair; designed by the authors, 1986; project.

The two models shown here represent two design phases; the first is pictured in Figures 11-39, 11-40.

Both the 1:4 scale model (Figs. 11-39, 11-40) and the full-size model (Fig. 11-41) were made of paper and wood.

The small scale model was made entirely of colored three-ply paper with the exception of the legs, which were made of basswood. The model was collapsible and had moving parts; the hinges were made with straight pins cut to size.

The full-size model was not a development of the first idea but a successive design step. The new concept was derived from an existing product of the client's. In redesigning this product we probably dared too much; our client did not feel ready to risk the heavy investment for the equipment required by our design.

11-39

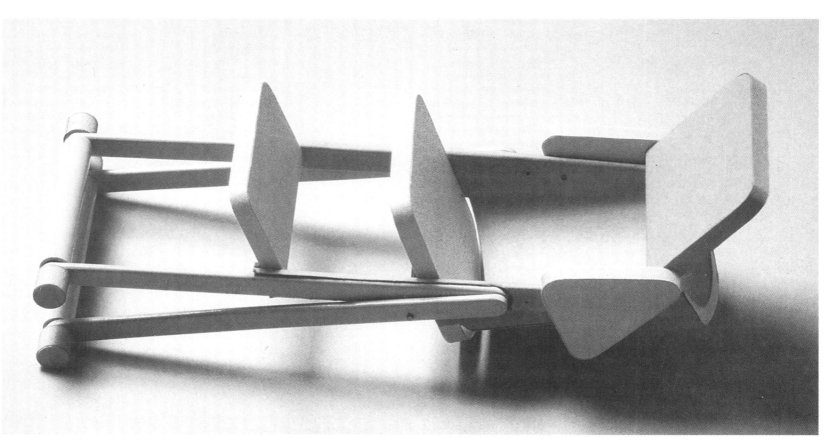

11-40

The full-size model, although in paper, had moving parts: The serving tray was removable and could slide back and forth; the seat could be adjusted to different heights. The buttons that locked the height control and the slide-off movement of the serving tray were made of red three-ply paper.

The star base was fitted with real casters. A hardwood frame was concealed inside the star base and the slanted post; the covering was made with white three-ply paper. The seat and the tray were made of foamcore covered with white three-ply paper.

Note the logo, cut from a brochure following the contours of the letters and glued onto a piece of cardboard to obtain a three-dimensional effect.

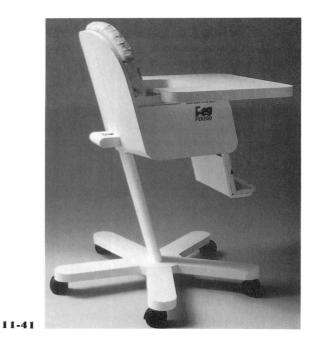

11-41

FIGURE **11-42**

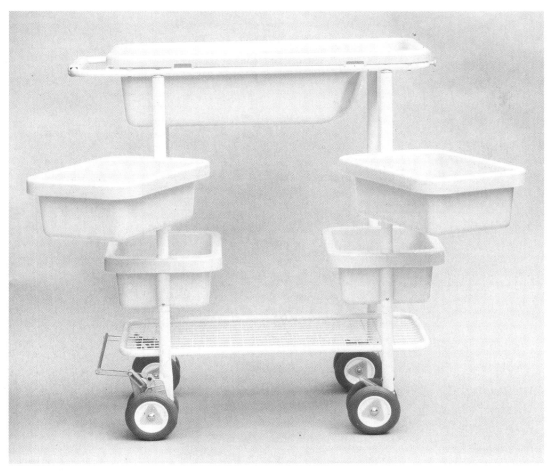

11-42

Baby's bath trolley, "Baby Toilette"; designed by the authors, 1987; manufactured by Peg Perego Pines, Arcore (Milan), Italy.

Since the company is probably the world's most important stroller manufacturer, we had the idea of designing a product that uses the typical soft stroller wheels to make the baby's bath easy to move from nursery to bathroom. An easy-to-operate pedal brake keeps the cart firmly in position during the bath.

An added ergonomic feature is provided by the four movable plastic containers for bath products and clothing. They can be positioned all around the caregiver, thus allowing easy access to all the necessary objects.

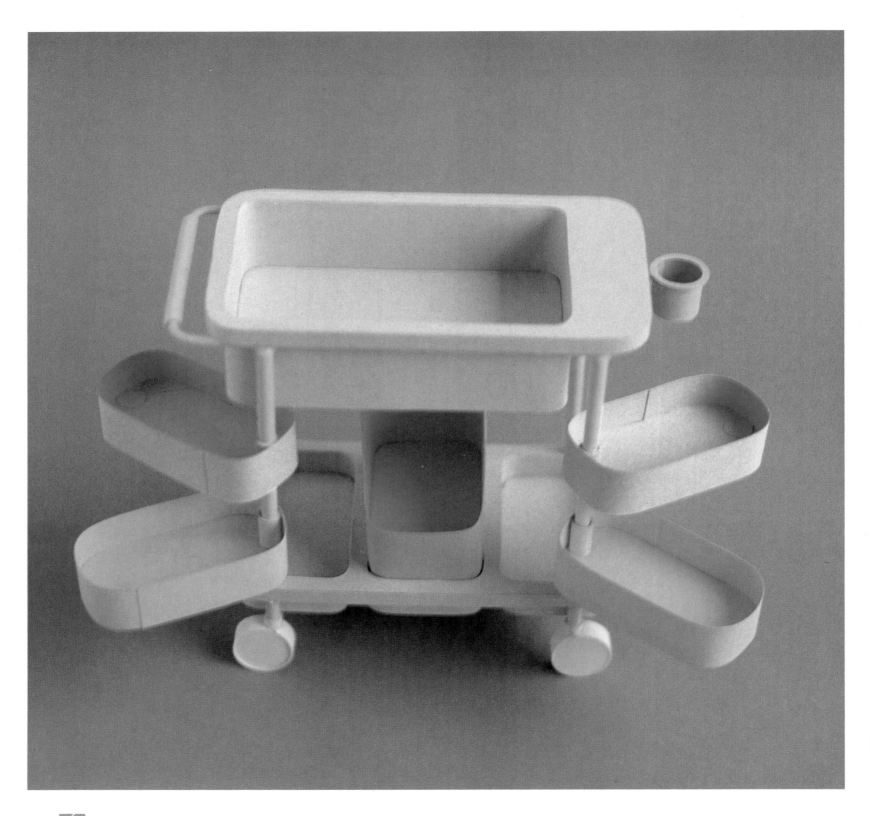

FIGURE **11-43**

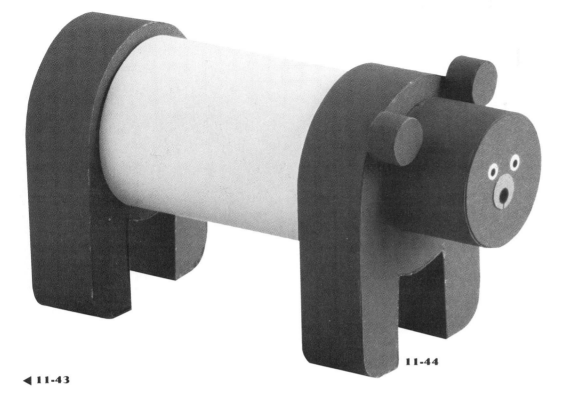

◄ **11-43**

11-44

Baby's bath trolley, "Baby Toilette."

The 1:10 scale model, which can also be seen in Figure 10-7, was built of colored two-ply paper and ⅛-inch (3mm) PVC dowels. The purpose of this model was to show the client the first design concept. A 1:1 scale model was then built out of paper, utilizing a metal tube frame supplied by the client.

FIGURES 11-44, 11-45

11-45

Modular toy; designed by the authors, 1985; project.

These stylized animals could be assembled by the child properly or improperly (the head of the lion with the legs of the bear; or the head upside down) on a musical body that was the same for all the animals (the white cylinder). The 1:1 scale modular model was made entirely of colored three-ply paper.

11-46

11-47

11-48

Reed organ for children, "2255"; designed by the authors, 1984; manufactured by Antonelli, Osimo (Ancona), Italy.

The real product is shown in Figure 11-46. The 1:1 scale model (Fig. 11-47) was built of foamcore covered with yellow three-ply paper. For the handle and the textured top, see Special Effects, Chapter 1. Other details can be seen in Figures 1-40 and 1-41. The keyboard and on/off button were supplied by the manufacturer.

FIGURES 11-48, 11-49

Portable electric reed organ, "2310"; designed by the authors, 1982; manufactured by Antonelli, Osimo (Ancona), Italy.

The real product is pictured in Figure 11-48; the full-size model in Figure 11-49. The model was built of foamcore covered with colored three-ply paper; the six major chords were made with red three-ply paper backed with black paper, as described for LEDs in Special Effects, Chapter 1. The main keyboard was supplied by the manufacturer.

11-49

11-50

Electronic organ, "2415"; designed by the authors, 1979; manufactured by Antonelli, Osimo (Ancona), Italy.

The real product is pictured in Figure 11-50; the full-size model in Figure 11-51. The model was made with black four-ply paper; foamcore was used only for the ribbings (or bulkheads) placed at the ends of the model and under the grooves. The keyboard is completely two-dimensional, made with black and white paper strips.

11-51

11-52

11-53

Navigation computer, "Geonav"; designed by the authors, 1986; manufactured by Navionics, Viareggio (Lucca), Italy.

This electronic unit was designed to endure the conditions aboard fishing and leisure boats; sturdiness and resistance to sun and water were the main concerns.

The case is molded in rigid expanded polyurethane. The membrane keyboard is waterproof and angled slightly for better ergonomics.

The 1:1 scale model (Fig. 11-53) was built entirely of foamcore covered with black three-ply paper. The photo was deliberately overexposed (see Exposure, Chapter 9) in order to show the dark details under the screen. The textured surface of the back part of the case was made as described in Special Effects, Chapter 1. Note that our graphic design for the keyboard is quite different from that of the real product; we were not responsible for the graphic design of the latter. The model's keyboard and the map simulation on the screen were made with transfer lettering, drawn in ink, reproduced, photographically reversed (to read white on black), printed, and colored with markers.

11-54

FIGURE **11-54**

Navigation computer, "Geonav."

A new version of the unit shown in Figures 11-52 and 11-53 was developed one year later. The features of the new design were a wider screen and a different keyboard arrangement. The paper 1:1 scale model of the front part was built like the model described in Figure 11-53 (the back was taken from a standard production "Geonav"). The keyboard was obtained from a photograph of the "Geonav's" existing graphics; the keys were cut out individually and glued onto the model.

11-55

FIGURES 11-55, 11-56

11-56

Navigation computer, "Micronav"; designed by the authors, 1987; manufactured by Navionics, Viareggio (Lucca), Italy.

The family of navigation computers was completed with the design of a smaller, more economical model, better suited for small boats (11-56).

The 1:1 scale model was built with the same materials as the models shown in Figures 11-53 and 11-54. The back part of the case was not textured, however, since it was supposed to represent sheet metal instead of molded rigid polyurethane foam. The keyboard was also made in a different way: The keys were individually cut from colored two-ply paper and glued onto dark gray three-ply paper. An 8-inch CRT screen was supplied by the client and encased in the model.

11-57

Stereophonic color television sets, "Logos" and "Stratos"; designed by the authors, 1986; manufactured by Brionvega, Milan, Italy.

Two of a series of television sets designed with a modular concept: A common screen frame module can be mounted on different cabinets. (Photo: Roberto Gennari)

11-58

FIGURES 11-59, 11-60, 11-61

11-59

11-60

Stereophonic color television sets, "Logos" and "Stratos"; 1:5 scale models.

The modular concept described for Figures 11-57 and 11-58 is expressed in this small modular model, which can be considered a three-dimensional sketch.

The cabinet models were made by laminating together two sheets of black three-ply paper and one sheet of colored three-ply paper. We selected papers of the same weight and thickness in order to build a strong lamination that would not warp. The central module was built out of black three-ply paper and the glass covering of the CRT was symbolically represented by a piece of glossy black two-ply paper.

11-61

11-62

Control panel for sports cars; designed by the authors, 1983; project.

Two versions of an electronic modular control panel. Instruments were placed on individual modules, which could then be assembled in different ways on various types of cars.

The models were built, module by module, in black three-ply paper and assembled on a foamcore base. The graphics were made with transfer type and symbols. In order to have the instrument dials printed in negative, we photographed the originals and printed the inverted negative. The white spaces of the negative prints were eventually colored with markers.

11-63

Control desk for polyurethane molding equipment; designed by the authors, 1987; manufactured by Afros Cannon, Caronno Pertusella (Varese), Italy; 1:4 scale model.

This electronic desk, to be operated by a standing person, consists of two keyboards and a monitor (CRT); these components are mounted on a rigid polyurethane foam casing. A sheet-metal cabinet houses all the power equipment and is the pedestal for the upper part of the unit.

The CRT without its protective tinted glass (bottom left: a two-sheet lamination of glossy black two-ply paper) can be seen in Figure 11-64. The CRT screen was simulated with silver-finish paper.

The keyboards were drawn in ink on colored one-ply paper and glued with rubber cement onto foamcore panels covered with black three-ply paper. Clear acetate protective screens ($1/64$ inch/0.4mm thick) were placed on the keyboards.

11-64

11-65

11-66

11-67

Control desk for polyurethane molding equipment; phases of the model-making process.

The foamcore parts are shown in Figure 11-66; note the two vertical black stripes on the pedestal, made with a marker; they represented grooves and gaskets in the finished model (see Fig. 1-51 and Special Effects, Chapter 1).

Figure 11-67 shows the gray and black three-ply paper coverings before they are glued to the foamcore parts of the base.

Figure 11-68 shows the partly covered console with its black three-ply paper covering before it is glued to the foamcore structure.

11-68

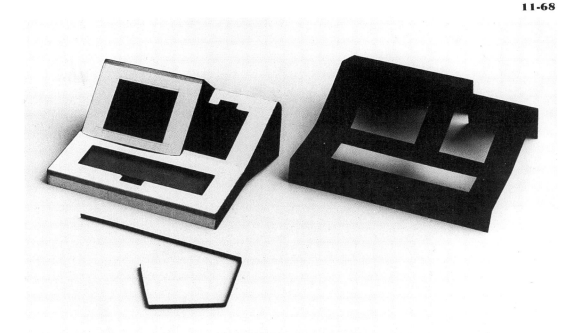

FIGURE 11-69

Control desk for polyurethane molding equipment; 1:1 scale mock-up.

This mock-up, of triple-faced corrugated board, was made for checking the ergonomics (position of keyboards and screen) of the console.

FIGURE 11-70

Electronic counter scale, "Pulsar BE 40"; designed by the authors, 1983; manufactured by Zenith, Milan, Italy.

The top part of the scale with the keyboard and display can be adjusted to the height of the counter by means of a simple and colorful device: As many as three colored plastic spacers can be inserted in the unit's stem, allowing for various heights.

11-70

◀ 11-69

11-71

11-72

  EXAMPLES

11-73

Electronic counter scale, "Pulsar BE 40"; 1:3 scale models.

The three models represent three different design options requested by the client as a result of three different marketing analyses.

The models were made of foamcore covered with black and silver-finish two-ply paper. The thin stem of the second design (Fig. 11-72) was a piece of balsa wood with a **D**-shaped section (see Making a Round Shape, Chapter 3) and painted black. The graphics were made with white transfer lettering. Note in the first design (Fig. 11-71) the small squares and dots made out of colored one-ply paper that imitate LEDs and similar luminescent displays.

FIGURE **11-74**

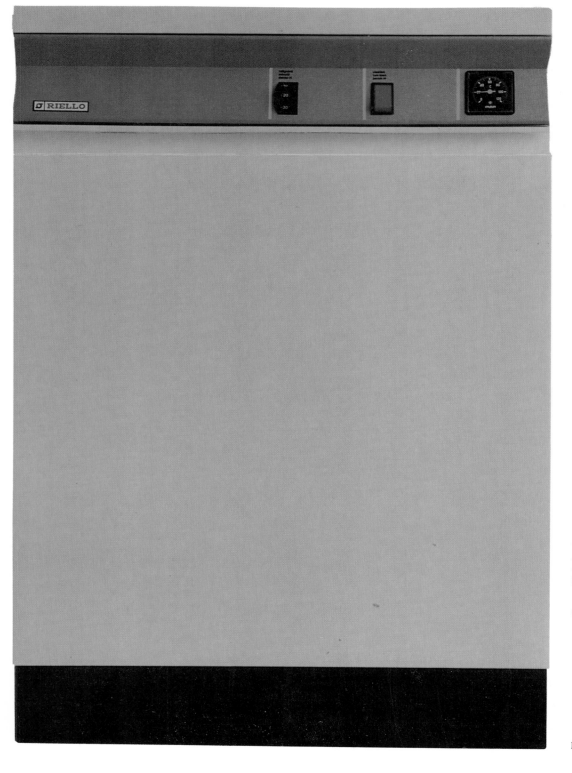

Gas heater, "RMC"; designed by the authors, 1985; manufactured by Riello, Legnago (Verona), Italy; 1:1 scale panel model.

This and other similar "flat" models (Figs. 11-75 to 11-79) belong to a group that can be called panel models; they are simple but often detailed models that represent only the front of the unit. It is a fast yet effective way to build models that show only the most interesting (from the point of view of design) part of the product.

It is important to note that in this and other similar cabinetlike products, the design job often concentrates on the control panel. The mass market usually does not allow for revolutionary changes.

The big white panel was made out of foamcore covered with white three-ply paper; the control panel from colored three-ply paper. The switch and the thermometer are real and were supplied by the manufacturer; the thermostat (center) was made with a strip of black two-ply paper, decorated with white lettering, shaped into a half cylinder, and glued onto a rectangular piece of black three-ply paper. The entire assemblage was then glued in position onto the control panel.

Note the emblem at left; it was made as described under Emblems, Chapter 8.

11-74

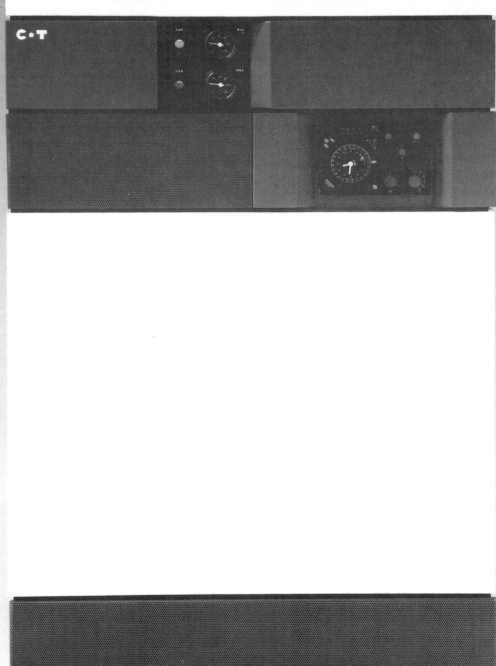

Gas heater and boiler, "MG/K"; designed by the authors, 1987; manufactured by Kalard, Piombino Dese (Padua), Italy; full-size panel models.

This model is similar to the one in Figure 11-74. The first design solution is shown in Figures 11-75 and 11-76. The main feature, and the main difference between it and the further design development (Fig. 11-77), is the perforated aluminum paneling. To match the color of the perforated metal panels we painted the four-ply paper control panels too, a difficult job we do not normally recommend.

The thermometers, thermostat, and timer are real pieces supplied by the manufacturer. The two pilot lights were made as described in Special Effects: LEDs, Chapter 1; round black and white transfer lines were added to simulate highlights and reflected shades.

11-75

11-76

11-77

Details of the control panel and the small door that conceals the temperature control knobs and switches can be seen in Figure 11-76.

The final version is shown in Figure 11-77. For safety reasons it was necessary to use a grille instead of perforated metal; in the model, the grille was made by assembling white three-ply paper laminated panels.

FIGURE **11-78**

Built-in electric oven; designed by the authors, 1985; manufactured by Candy, Monza (Milan), Italy; 1:1 scale panel model.

We used foamcore covered with white three-ply paper with gray and black two-ply paper for the strips decorating the oven door. The horizontal bars were made from foamcore wrapped with white two-ply paper. The ⅛-inch (3mm) radius of the bar profile was made as described in Scoring for Bending, Chapter 1.

The knobs are cylinders made out of white three-ply paper, to which graphics were added using transfer lettering. The logo was obtained from a photocopy of a company's brochure (see Logos, Chapter 8).

11-78

FIGURE **11-79**

Washing machine; designed by the authors, 1983; manufactured by Zerowatt, Nese (Bergamo), Italy; 1:1 scale panel model.

As we have said, the design of products such as this washing machine is usually concentrated on the control panel and on a few other front details. In this case we decided on a modular design because the company was planning to produce several models with different features, all having basically the same panel but with a different number of knobs and buttons. The modular design was emphasized by the surface's geometric texture. The company eventually manufactured a simpler version of this design.

The paper model was made out of foamcore covered with white, black, and colored three-ply paper. The texture of the control panel was made by gluing three-ply paper squares onto a three-ply paper surface, as explained in Special Effects, Chapter 1. The graphics were made with transfer lettering.

11-79

11-80

FIGURE 11-80

Wall-mounted gas boiler heater; designed by the authors, 1988; manufactured by Riello, Legnago (Verona), Italy; full-size model.

The model was made entirely of foamcore and covered with white three-ply paper. The thermometer and pressure gauge were made of one-ply drawing paper decorated with transfer lettering and covered (after a black paper separator ring was interposed) with clear acetate. The knobs were made by laminating white two-ply paper to obtain rigid, plasticlike forms. The switches are real.

A further version of the control panel can be seen in Figure 8-1.

FIGURES 11-81, 11-82

11-81

11-82

Portable air-conditioning unit, "ET 9"; designed by the authors, 1987; manufactured by Ricagni, Milan, Italy.

This air-conditioning unit can easily be transported from one room to another. The main design idea was to make the object as unobtrusive as possible (note its flat, geometric shape and the clear plastic air duct).

The 1:1 scale model (Fig. 11-82) was built in foamcore and covered with colored three-ply paper. The transparent air duct was built out of clear PVC ($\frac{1}{32}$ inch/ 0.8mm thick). To assemble the air duct we used clear polyester tape instead of glue (see Adhesives, Chapter 5).

Details of this model can be seen in Figures 1-62 and 1-64.

11-83

Air-conditioning unit, "Fancoil Split"; designed by the authors, 1988; manufactured by Ricagni, Milan, Italy.

The unit's large grille surface makes the airflow particularly silent. The control panel (Fig. 11-83, top right) can be removed and placed in a more convenient place somewhere in the room. A description of the control panel's graphics, which can also be mounted on other units, can be seen in Figures 8-16 to 8-20.

The first 1:3 scale paper model (foamcore and colored three-ply paper covering) is shown in Figure 11-84. A second model of the same unit can be seen in Figure 1-50.

The final model built in wood by a professional model-maker is shown in Figure 11-85. To save time, the model-maker accepted our suggestions to imitate the grille's openings with black adhesive foil strips (see Figs. 1-50 and 1-64), instead of making a real grille. (Photos 11-83, 11-85: Gianni Ghezzi)

11-84

11-85

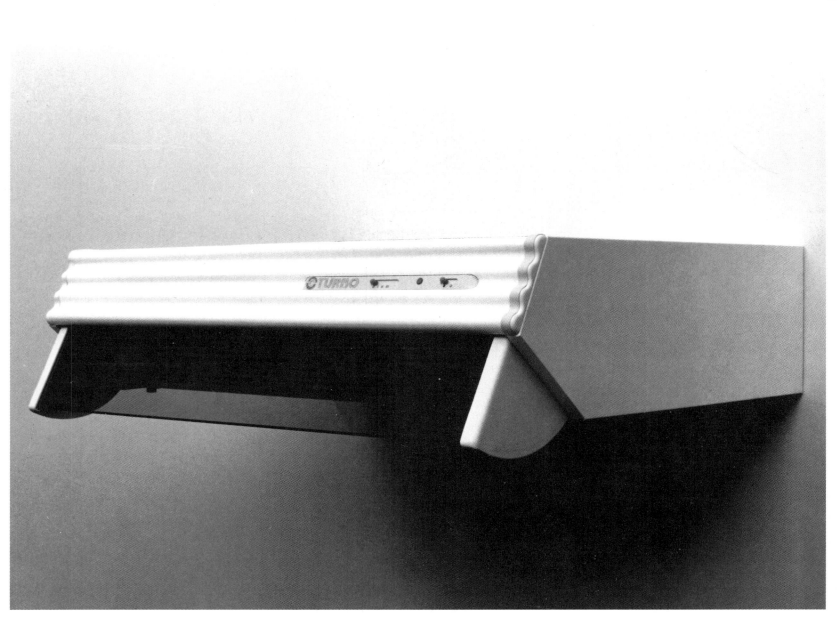

11-86

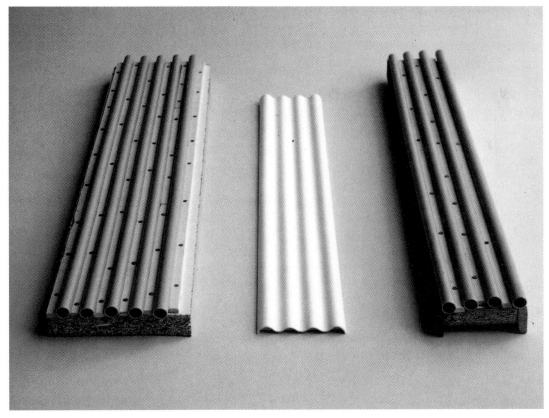

11-87

Kitchen range hood; designed by the authors, 1986; project; 1:1 scale model.

The problem was to redesign the front only, to give the product a new look, while keeping the larger and less visible part of the unit the way it was. This would have enabled the company to save considerably on the cost of equipment.

We built a model that utilized all of the unit's sheet-metal casing and we made a new front panel out of three laminated sheets of white three-ply paper (Fig. 11-87). At the ends of the laminated panel we glued two balsa wood caps (see Spherical Forms, Chapter 1). Note the strip of gray paper; it helped to disguise the connection between the white paper and the wood detail. This same aesthetic device was to be used for the real product, since the corrugated panel was sheet metal and the caps were plastic.

We covered the existing metal casing with white three-ply paper and placed a control panel incorporating the emblem onto the laminated paper panel (see Special Effects, Chapter 1; Names and Emblems, Chapter 8).

11-88

11-90

11-91

Kitchen range hood; designed by the authors, 1987; project; 1:1 scale models.

As a further development of the design seen in Figure 11-86 we offered the client two new front design options, using a common cabinet. The basic functional element, the cabinet, was made of foamcore covered with white three-ply paper. We could not use the existing metal casing because it was slightly different in size from that of the new design.

The small control panels on both models were made with white three-ply paper; for the details, see Figure 11-86 and the corresponding text in Chapters 1 and 8. The grille openings were drawn in ink and filled in with a black marker.

We did not make two entire models; rather, we made one basic model with different front details and showed our client photographs only. In this way the model-making process was similar to the real production process, insofar as the metal casing is the same for more than one model, whereas the style of the front panel varies.

Figures 11-90 and 11-91 picture 1:1 scale "technical" models made to show the company's technical staff our modular design concept; these were constructed primarily from white four-ply paper.

A bronzed polymethyl-methacrylate sheet was used instead of tinted glass. The L-shaped detail made of balsa wood (Figs. 11-90, 11-91, foreground) represented a plastic cap designed to be a joint between the front and the main part of the unit. This added piece would have provided a soft look to sheet metal corners, much as balsa details can soften the edges of paper corners (see Spherical Forms, Chapter 1).

11-92

Drinking glasses; designed by the authors, 1986; project; 1:1 scale models.

The models shown in Figure 11-92 were made of glossy black two-ply paper. The inside of the glasses (the back face of glossy paper is usually white) was colored with a black marker.

Note that the shape of these models was obtained simply by folding the paper, without any internal structure.

The quick models in Figure 11-93 were made of $\frac{1}{64}$-inch (0.4mm) clear acetate. The material was used like paper, the shape obtained by overlapping the cut-out acetate sheets and fixing them with clear polyester tape to form a conical or cylindrical shape.

These Figures show similar designs represented in two different media. In our view, although the paper models have a more abstract look, they are nevertheless more elegant than the acetate ones. The paper models also allow for a better evaluation of the shape.

11-93

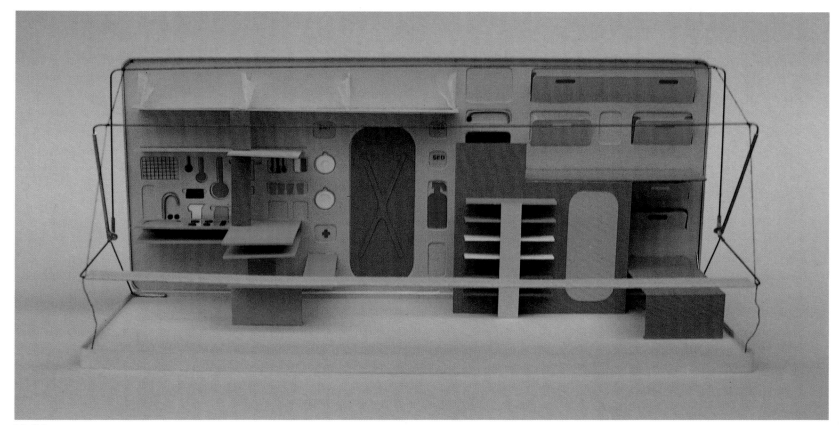

11-94

FIGURES 11-94, 11-95, 11-96

Collapsible house, "Book-House"; designed by the authors, 1987; sponsored by Plaxil, Osoppo (Udine), Italy; 1:20 scale model

This paper model was made for the exhibition entitled "I Segni dell'Habitat, Italian Technology and Design" (Paris, France, 1987).

"Book-House" was a ready-to-use house with everything included: plumbing, wiring, kitchen equipment, beds, housewares. The house folded flat, and many of them stacked next to each other easily could be transported, by truck or by train, to holiday resorts or to disaster areas where emergency housing was needed.

The model consisted of two foamcore panels covered on both sides with two sheets of laminated colored paper. The exterior sheet of each panel had windows cut out with the contour of folding shelves, cabinet doors, and various household items; all these items could fit into the cut-out recessed shapes. Doors and shelves were made of laminated colored three-ply paper. Tables, chairs, beds, and bathroom walls were also of laminated colored three-ply paper. The hinges connecting the two foamcore panels were made of two-ply paper.

A metal frame suggested the idea of a vinyl covering for walls and roof that would work like the roof of a convertible car. The frame was built from aluminum tubing (⅛ inch/3mm in diameter) and piano wire (1/16 inch/1.5mm thick).

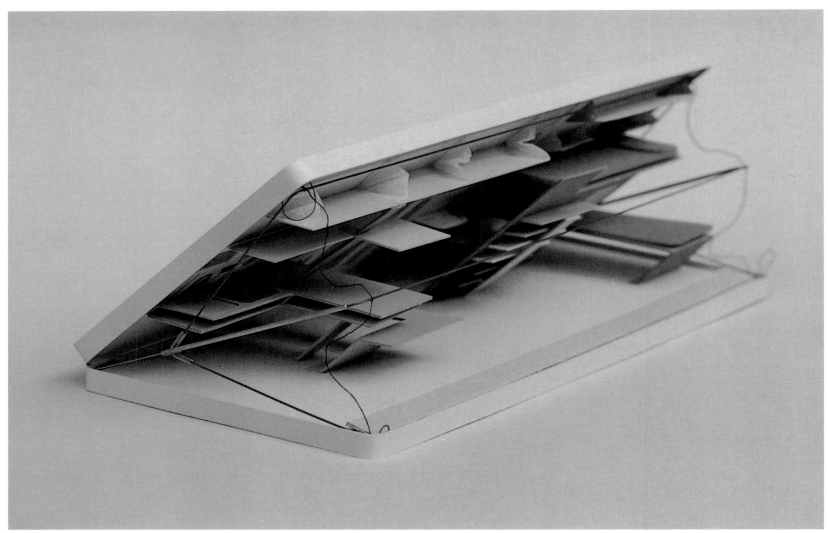

11-95

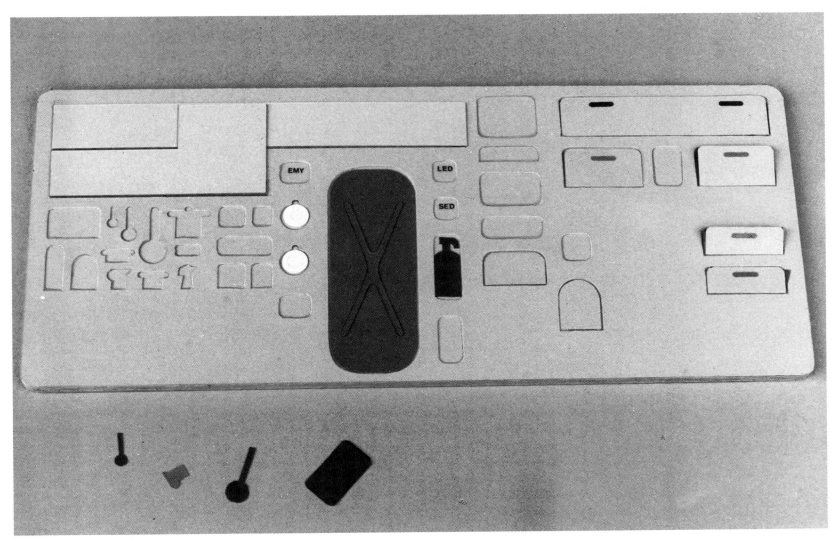

11-96

FIGURES 11-97, 11-98

11-97

11-98

Public seating; designed by Riccardo Dall'Acqua, Guido Lanci, Serafin Rodriguez, Emanuele Soldini, Laura Whitby—fourth-year students, academic year 1985–86; Industrial Design Department, Istituto Europeo di Design, Milan, Italy; Roberto Lucci and Paolo Orlandini, instructors; Karim Azzabi, assistant; sponsor: La Magona d'Italia, Florence, Italy.

The aim of this project was to promote the use of precoated sheet metal, the material produced by the sponsor. The full-size prototype of the seat shown in Figure 11-97 was built in precoated sheet metal with rigid polyurethane foam sandwiched inside. The two caps at the ends of the sheet-metal seat were designed to be injection molded in plastic. The pedestal, also serving the function of the arm, was cast in concrete.

The 1:4 scale model (Fig. 11-98) was made of colored three-ply paper; the seat caps were balsa wood and the base extruded polystyrene foam. (Photos: Emanuele Soldini)

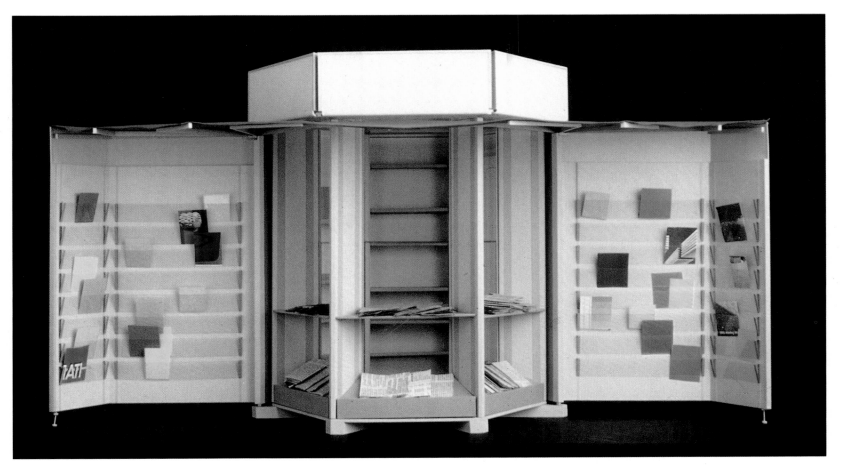

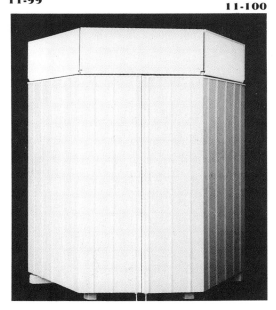

11-99

11-100

FIGURES 11-99, 11-100

Newsstand; designed by Pedro Arietta Garate, Daniele Bresciani, Luis Heriz Ormaechea, Pierluigi Meneghetti, Paolo Ramorino—fourth-year students, academic year 1985–86; Industrial Design Department, Istituto Europeo di Design, Milan, Italy; Roberto Lucci and Paolo Orlandini, instructors; Karim Azzabi, assistant; sponsor: La Magona d'Italia, Florence, Italy; 1:5 scale model.

The project was part of the same promotional program described in Figures 11-97 and 11-98; therefore almost everything was to be made of precoated sheet metal.

The model had moving parts and was built of foamcore and colored three-ply paper; the magazine holders were clear acetate; the folding roof was made of cotton shirt fabric; and its structure was made with hardwood sticks. (Photos: Roberto Facciolla)

FIGURE **11-101**

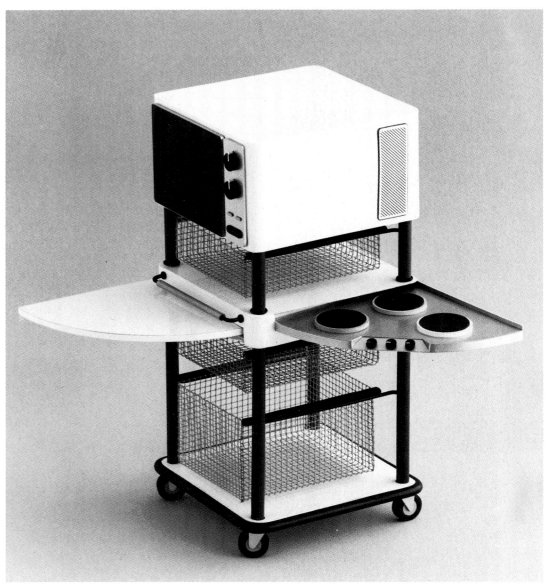

11-101

Portable kitchen unit; designed by Valeria Bonucchi and Antonella Ortelli—fourth-year students, academic year 1983–84; Industrial Design Department, Istituto Europeo di Design, Milan, Italy; Roberto Lucci and Paolo Orlandini, instructors; Riccardo Zarino, assistant; sponsor: Candy, Monza (Milan), Italy; 1:4 scale model.

The design consists of two basic subunits: the lower part, with two welded mesh containers, a pullout table, and three electric heating elements; the upper part, with another mesh container and a microwave oven with a built-in filter extractor.

The model, with moving parts, was built using plastic dowels for the structure; foamcore covered with glossy two-ply paper, for the oven and table-range container; real metal welded mesh, for the baskets. The details were either found objects (toy wheels, electrical wire, rubber O-rings) or expressly made plastic parts (knobs sliced from a dowel, heating units cut from a polystyrene sheet). The oven's grille was very heavy Bristol cardboard (1/16 inch/1.6mm) covered with a self-adhesive pattern (Letratone). The oven door was made of glossy black two-ply paper to imitate tinted glass. (Photo: Roberto Facciolla)

FIGURE **11-102**

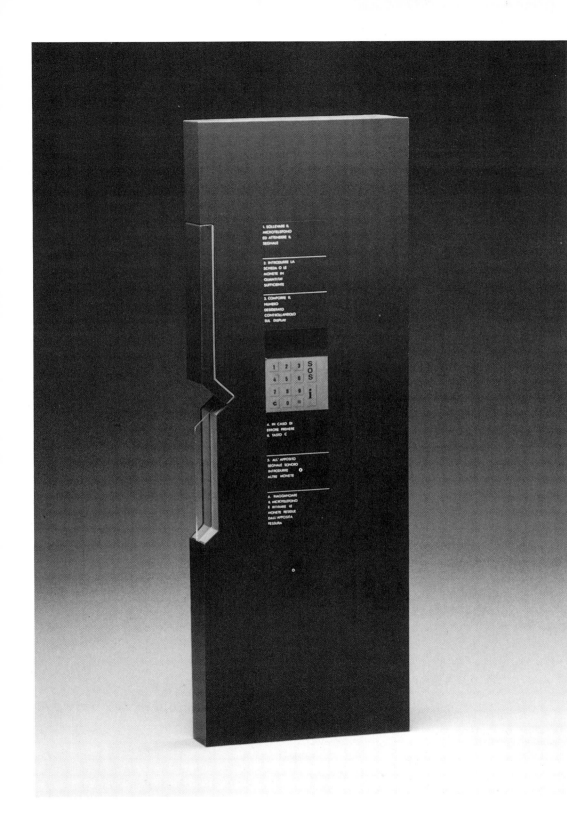

Public telephone set; designed by Betta Gaudenzi, Serafin Rodriguez, Emanuele Soldini—third-year students, academic year 1984–85; Industrial Design Department, Istituto Europeo di Design, Milan, Italy; Paolo Bistacchi, instructor; full-size model.

The upper part of the broken edge of this pure geometric design is the detachable handset (also in the model). The keyboard is the membrane type.

The model was made of foamcore covered with colored three-ply paper. A small piece of clear polymethyl-methacrylate was fitted under the handset. The graphics were made with transfer lettering. (Photo: Emanuele Soldini)

11-102

12-1

FIGURE 12-1

Ergonomic chair, "Movia"; designed by the authors, 1985; manufactured by Fantoni, Osoppo (Udine), Italy; 1:1 scale model of seat and backrest.

This expanded polystyrene model was made for checking the upholstery to be mounted on some of the versions of the "Movia" chair.

We used the most commonly available expanded polystyrene (1.9 pounds per cubic foot/30kg per m³ density); the material was cut with a hot-wire cutter; edges were softened and the shape was refined with sanding pads.

The textured surface at the center of both the seat and the backrest was created by individually working the single elements and then gluing them in position. Water-based paint was used for finishing the model.

12-2

FIGURE 12-2

Desk chair; designed by the authors, 1981; project; 1:1 scale model of seat and backrest.

The design of this office chair was characterized by a very high and narrow backrest, the ideal solution for providing extended support to the spine and freedom of movement to the arms. Unfortunately this concept does not meet with the design standards for office chairs.

The model was made in three separate parts (seat, side panels, and backrest) from expanded polystyrene. The two knobs at the back of the seat were meant to be controls for inclining the backrest and adjusting the height of the seat. They were made of balsa wood.

Chair, "Billy"; designed by the authors, 1980; manufactured by Sesta, Massalengo (Milan), Italy.

This economical stacking chair has a metal tube frame and a plastic seat and backrest. Both the seat and the backrest snap onto the metal frame without fasteners.

The expanded polystyrene (1.9 pounds per cubic foot/30kg per m^3 density) model of the plastic seat and backrest is shown in Figure 12-4. The geometric texture was engraved into the foam surface with a sandpaper tool made from a piece of thin plywood ($^1/_{16}$ inch/1.5mm thick) sandwiched between two pieces of 100-grit abrasive paper (see Sanding and Finishing Tools, Chapter 2).

12-3

12-4

12-5

12-6

12-7

12-8

FIGURES 12-5, 12-6, 12-7, 12-8

Desk chair; designed by the authors, 1986; project; 1:4 scale models.

Two of the consecutive design solutions can be seen in Figures 12-5 and 12-6. The models' structures and star bases were made of laminated paper (four sheets of three-ply paper). The upholstery was made of two sheets of ⁵⁄₆₄-inch-thick (2mm) expanded polyethylene with an inner laminated paper part (Figs. 12-7, 12-8). A ³⁄₈-inch (10mm) PVC dowel, cut to size, was used to make the casters.

12-9

12-10

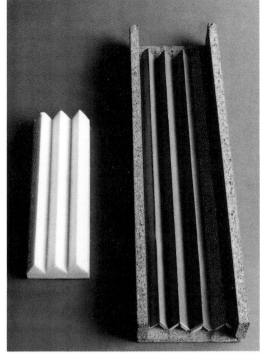

12-11

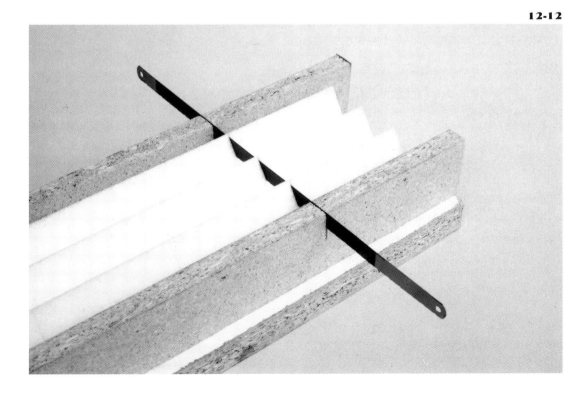

12-12

Air-conditioning unit; designed by the authors, 1988; project; 1:1 scale panel model.

This model belongs to the category of panel models described in Figure 11-74; the cabinet was supplied by the client and we had to design only the front. The model was made of rigid polyurethane foam.

The removable electronic control unit shown in Figure 12-9 can be seen in detail in Figures 8-16 to 8-20.

As shown in Figure 12-10, the upper part of the grille has movable modules to direct the airflow. The grille's openings were simulated with black paper, as described in Special Effects, Chapter 1.

Some steps of the model-making process can be seen in Figures 12-11 and 12-12; note the special sandpaper tool shown at right in Figure 12-11 (see Sanding and Finishing Tools, Chapter 2). A precision cutting system is shown in Figure 12-12.

12-13

Car interior; designed by Karim Azzabi, Floriano Godoy, Juan Andres Montesa, Lucy Leon Salamenca, Massimo Siena—fourth-year students, academic year 1984–85; Industrial Design Department, Istituto Europeo di Design, Milan, Italy; Roberto Lucci and Paolo Orlandini, instructors; Riccardo Zarino, assistant; sponsor: Alfa Romeo, Milan, Italy; full-size model.

The interiors shown in Figures 12-13 to 12-15 were parallel projects developed by two groups of students, following the specifications given by the marketing department of Alfa Romeo. The interior shown in Figure 12-13 was intended for a youthful market.

This interior, like the one shown in Figure 12-15, was built by the students directly inside the empty body of an Alfa 33.

Polymethacrylimid rigid foam was employed for the steering wheel, air vents, instrument panel, and radio. Other details were made of hardwood dowels and plywood. The seats were constructed of expanded polystyrene and covered with fabric. The embossed Alfa Romeo emblem on the steering wheel was cut out from a $\frac{1}{16}$-inch-thick (1.5mm) PVC sheet. The logo on the dashboard was cut out from four-ply paper and then covered with fabric. The door panels were made of foamcore covered with fabric.

12-14

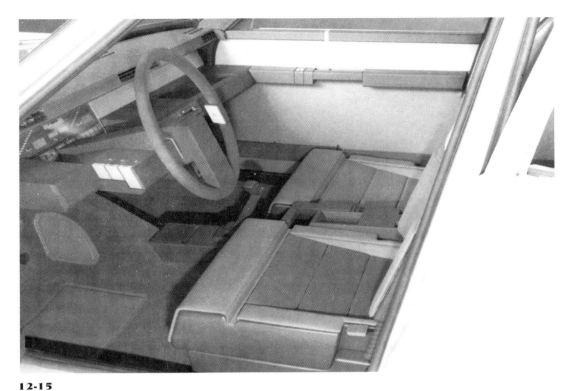

12-15

FIGURE **12-15**

Car interior; designed by Adewale Adebayo, Fabio Falange, Angel Marti Prieto, Francesco Nicastro, Maria Mercedes Rodriguez, Alessio Verin—fourth-year students, academic year 1984–85; Industrial Design Department, Istituto Europeo di Design, Milan, Italy; Roberto Lucci and Paolo Orlandini, instructors; Riccardo Zarino, assistant; sponsor: Alfa Romeo, Milan, Italy; full-size model.

This interior, in comparison to the previous one, was designed for an older, more conservative market.

Polymethacrylimid rigid foam was used for the dashboard, steering wheel, gearshift, and armrests; ⅛-inch-thick (3mm) PVC sheet was used for the buttons and similar details; expanded polystyrene was used for the inside of the seats, fabric for their covering, and painted plywood for their side panels. The door panels were made of foamcore covered with colored three-ply paper.

13-2

FIGURES 13-1, 13-2

Folding table "Caramella"; designed by the authors, 1984; manufactured by Ciatti, Badia a Settimo (Florence), Italy.

This ultralight folding table was designed for a company that specializes in hardwood furniture. The structure was designed to provide maximum strength with minimum material, in order to obtain a very light piece of furniture. This is, in our opinion, one of the main features a folding table should have. Metal braces stiffen the wooden structure and also work as part of the folding mechanism.

13-1

FIGURES 13-3, 13-4

13-3

Folding table, "Caramella"; working 1:4 scale model.

Note the border, which is much heavier than in the real product. After making this model we decided that a very thin border would have not only allowed us to make a lighter table, but also better communicated the idea of lightness.

The wooden frame was made from spruce strips; the tracks for the folding braces were made of aluminum sheets cut to size and bent. In the initial models the braces were made of wood. The colored dowels connecting the twin legs were made with electrical wire. The tabletop was made with very heavy Bristol cardboard, $1/16$ inch (1.6mm) thick.

13-4

13-5

13-6

FIGURE **13-5**

Folding table, "Caramella"; full-size paper model of the folding mechanism.

The brace and leg were made of foam-core covered with colored three-ply paper; the table border, track, and hinge were made of colored three-ply paper.

FIGURE 13-6

Folding chair, "Trio"; designed by the authors, 1986; manufactured by Calligaris, Manzano (Udine), Italy.

This folding chair was designed for a company that specializes in mass-produced wooden chairs. The three-leg option was selected to express the concept of a minimal chair and to achieve a simple, yet very strong folding mechanism. The weight of the sitting person is concentrated on the central leg, the strongest structural element of the chair.

An interesting aspect of the design is the bold graphic shape of the chair, when folded. In a folding chair it is important to carefully design both configurations of the chair: the open and the folded positions.

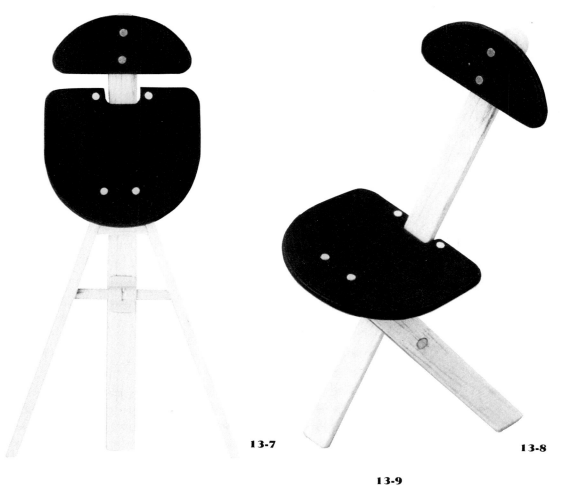

FIGURES 13-7, 13-8

Folding chair, "Trio"; first 1:5 scale model.

The model was made of balsa wood strips, black four-ply paper, and paper dots. The folding principle was already established, but the design was not yet well defined. Note the colored paper dots; with this first model we explored the possibilities of graphically solving a typical chair's design problem, the connecting elements between the seat and the main structure.

13-7

13-8

13-9

13-10

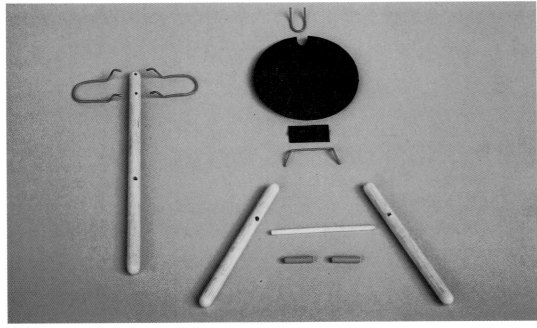

13-11

Folding chair, "Trio"; final 1:4 scale working model.

The model was made of balsa dowels, black four-ply paper, piano wire, and vinyl electrical wire insulation.

The legs' rounded section added elegance to the original design. At this stage, however, the backrest was uncomfortable; a plywood backrest was introduced in the first chair prototype.

13-12   **13-13**

Wooden chair system; designed by the authors, 1985; project.

This chair was developed for the same client as the "Trio" chair; the project consisted of a set of basic common elements and some interchangeable parts, thus originating a whole family of products. In consideration of the company's very large-scale production, we decided to design a system rather than a single chair.

The 1:4 scale models were collapsible and had interchangeable parts (see also Figs. 10-11 and 10-12). The legs were made of balsa wood dowels; the seats and backrests were either colored three-ply paper and piano wire, or balsa wood. The curved backrest of Figure 13-13 was made by laminating balsa sheets ($\frac{1}{32}$ inch/ 0.8mm thick) in the same way as paper is laminated (see Lamination, Chapter 1).

FIGURES 13-14, 13-15

13-14

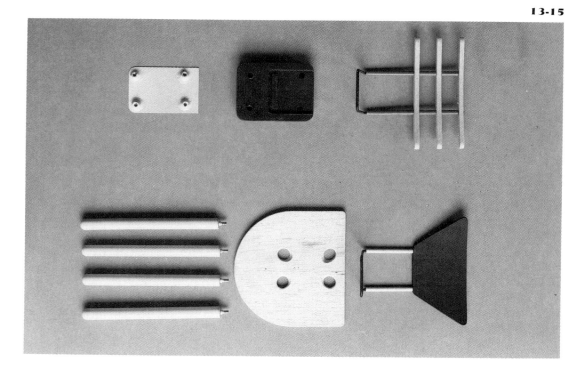

13-15

Wooden chair system; collapsible 1:4 scale model with interchangeable parts of the same chair system shown in Figures 13-12 and 13-13.

This new group of models was made to show in detail all the elements of the chairs as they would have been in the real product (which was never made).

The balsa legs had bits of screws inserted in their upper parts, glued to the wood with epoxy. The aluminum plate in the upper left corner of Figure 13-15 is the element that holds together the whole structure. Four nuts were glued with epoxy to the aluminum plate for holding the chair's legs, and filler was added to imitate drawn details on sheet metal. The piano wire parts were covered with vinyl electrical wire insulation.

FIGURE **13-16**

13-16

Modular cupboard and drawers; designed by the authors, 1978, project; 1:4 scale model.

The idea was to design an easy-to-assemble modular system of cupboards and drawers that could be used both at home and in the office. The materials would have been sheet metal for the shoulders and back; plywood for the tops, drawers, and doors. These pieces of furniture could have been assembled with drawers, doors, or open shelving, according to the user's desire.

The 1:4 scale model was built out of balsa sheets (⅛ inch/3mm thick) and black four-ply paper; it could be completely disassembled. Note the slots on the side panels; they are tracks for the drawers and would have been made from sheet metal with a simple bending operation.

13-17

FIGURE **13-17**

Executive desk; designed by the authors, 1986; project; 1:10 scale model.

The model utilized a walnut picture frame (a found object). Details were made of metal-finish paper. The black part of the desktop (textured black adhesive foil) could be tilted. A 1/16-inch-thick (1.5mm) piece of clear polymethyl-methacrylate covered part of the desktop and was flush with the wood sides. In the real desk it would have been a glass insert.

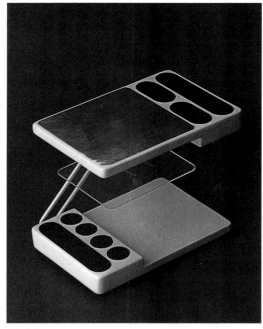

13-18

FIGURE **13-18**

Service cart; designed by the authors, 1973; project; 1:10 scale model.

This plastic folding cart with tubular structure was intended for use in the kitchen and dining room. The three planes fold parallel to each other with just one movement.

The folding model had two balsa wood planes; the middle plane was a piece of $\frac{1}{16}$-inch-thick (1.5mm) clear polymethylmethacrylate. Because of the small scale, adhesive foils were used to represent recessed areas, which would have been stainless steel and rubber pads in the real product.

13-19

FIGURE 13-19

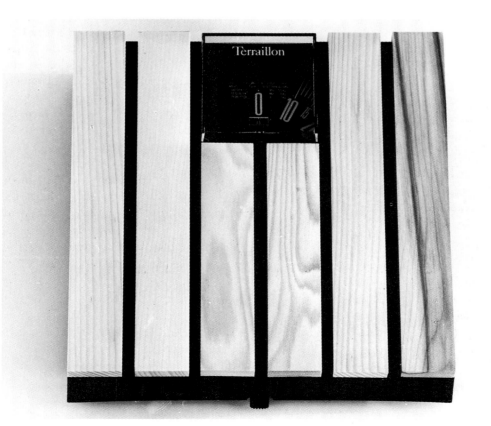

Bathroom scale, "T 1340"; designed by the authors, 1980; manufactured by Terraillon, Annemasse, France.

The design of this bathroom scale originated from the idea of having real wood as a surface for the user's naked feet, instead of plastic or other synthetic materials. Since the problem was to have a water-resistant surface at a reasonable cost, we decided to use small pieces of solid pine. Years later the company wanted to produce a less expensive version using plywood instead of solid wood. The result was a product that looked even cheaper than the price at which it was sold.

13-20

13-21

Bathroom scale, "T 1340." The 1:1 scale model was designed as a system model.

A single foamcore base covered with black four-ply paper was fitted with modularly spaced wooden pins to hold different wood patterns. We show only two of the many possible design options for the upper part of the scale. Clear polymethylmethacrylate (½ inch/12mm thick) was used to cover the dial flush with the natural wood pattern.

Not only were we able to show our client different designs, but the company itself could have easily manufactured a family of products with different wood patterns. The pieces of wood had to be small enough to be economical and they had to fit to the modular pins placed on the plastic (foamcore and black paper in the model) base of the scale. In this way the expensive part of the equipment for manufacturing the product would have been the same and would have allowed for more than one product to be manufactured.

Eventually the company decided to produce only one of the many options, mainly because during those years electronic bathroom scales were becoming more profitable while nonelectronic scales were being sold at ever lower prices. Nevertheless this scale was successful.

FIGURE 13-22

Plastic door handle; designed by the authors, 1983; project; 1:1 scale model.

The model was made of two pieces of balsa wood, painted separately and dry-assembled through two small wooden pegs.

FIGURE 13-23

13-22

13-23

Detector unit for electronic burglar alarm; designed by the authors, 1984; 1:1 aesthetic scale model.

The design basically consisted of a soft PVC case for an existing mechanism. Two types of models were necessary to show the design to the client: an aesthetic model and a functional one. The aesthetic model was built of balsa wood with details in glossy black paper and a red paper dot (the LED).

FIGURES 13-24, 13-25

Detector unit for electronic burglar alarm; functional 1:1 scale model.

The model, built to show the client the movements of the unit, was made of balsa wood blocks and tablets. Foam rubber pads were interposed between the balsa tablets; a piece of thick electrical wire connected all the elements, thus creating a flexible structure.

13-24

13-25

FIGURE 13-26

FIGURES 13-27, 13-28

Bicycle; designed by the authors, 1985; project; full-size model.

The idea was to design a supercompact bicycle that could be carried in the trunk of a compact car. In the model the plastic unitized body was made out of plywood. The wheels, crank arms, and pedals were taken from a child's bicycle and covered with black four-ply paper. For the seat post and the handlebar stem we used PVC tubing; the seat and handles were made of rigid polyurethane foam. The model was only aesthetic.

Polynesian sailing catamaran, "Proa 42"; designed by the authors, 1974; manufactured by Conaver, Biassono (Milan), Italy.

"Proa 42" has a Fiberglas hull and outrigger; overall length 14 feet (4.2m). The rigging, mast, beams, and outrigger all fit into the main hull for easy storage and transportation. The entire structure is mounted without metal fasteners, using only rope (the Polynesian way). (Metal fasteners are hard to replace if they break and they may cause injuries.) The rigging is very simple, and the boat has proved to be fast and safe.

◀ 13-26

13-27

13-28

13-29

FIGURE 13-29

Polynesian sailing catamaran, "Proa 42"; 1:10 scale model.

We used ⅛-inch (3mm) balsa sheets, laminated balsa beams, aluminum tubing for the mast, and cotton shirt fabric for the sail. The model was collapsible and could sail.

FIGURE 13-30

Sailing catamaran, "Artemide 1"; designed by the authors, 1976; sponsored by Artemide, Milan, Italy.

This 18-foot (5.5m) sailing catamaran was designed and built for the 1976 John Player World Sailing Speed Record. The hulls were plywood; the mast, beams, and special rigging were of aluminum.

13-30

FIGURE **13-31**

Sailing catamaran, "Artemide 1"; 1:10 scale model.

The hulls were made with ¹/₈-inch (3mm) balsa sheets; the mast, boom, and beams were aluminum tubing; the sail was light cotton shirt fabric. Note that the model was fitted with a special working rigging and could sail. Model boat rigging parts can easily be found at model shops.

13-31

FIGURE **13-32**

Sailing catamaran, "Artemide 2"; designed by the authors, 1979; sponsored by Artemide, Milan, Italy.

"Artemide 2" was designed for solo races and was characterized by an unusual oversized structure, necessary because solo navigation does not allow opportunities for repairs. The hulls were very thin to reduce weight and for maximizing the boat's performance. Overall length 30 feet (9m).

13-32

FIGURE **13-33**

Sailing catamaran, "Artemide 2"; 1:10 scale model.

The hulls were made with ⅛-inch-thick (3mm) balsa sheets; the structure was made from aluminum tubing joined with epoxy; the connecting elements between the structure and the hulls were made of piano wire 1/16 inch (1.5mm) thick; the sail and the tent were made of cotton shirt fabric.

13-33

FIGURE **13-34**

13-34

Sailing catamaran, "White Artemide"; designed by the authors, 1985; sponsored by Artemide, Milan, Italy.

A racing catamaran 38 feet (11.6m) long developed from the experience acquired with "Artemide 2." The concept of the minimal hulls was retained, while the central structure was noticeably improved and simplified. (Photo: Renato Polo)

FIGURE **13-35**

13-35

Sailing catamaran, "White Artemide"; 1:10 scale model.

Hulls, beams, and central nacelle were made of balsa sheets (⅛ inch/3mm thick); mast is aluminum tubing.

○ ○ ○ **METAL**

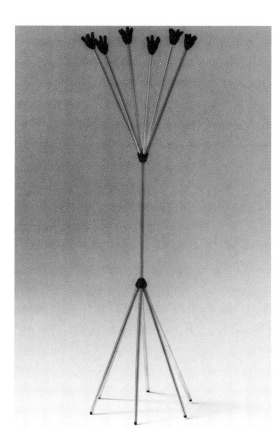

14-1

FIGURE 14-1

Coat-tree; designed by the authors, 1989; manufactured by Lamm, San Secondo Parmense, Italy; first presentation model (1:4 scale).

A very simple, low-priced coat-tree that can be assembled at home without using tools simply by plugging in its components. It consists of thirteen pieces of steel tubing and eight aluminum die-cast plugs that function as connecting elements as well as the hooks for hanging up coats. The model was made of aluminum tubing, balsa cones, and hardwood dowels.

FIGURE 14-2

14-2

Coat-tree: assembling the aluminum tubes of the scale model (see Assembling and Gluing, Chapter 3).

Note the nail at the center of the foam-core base for checking the geometry of this part of the model.

The six aluminum tubes were bonded together with epoxy; a balsa cap was later glued on top of the tube pyramid. The pieces were braced with drafting tape and foamcore base. The assembly of the model was different from that of the real product. The small dimensions of the model and the precise geometry of the design made it impossible to make a dismountable model while maintaining the desired geometry.

14-3   **FIGURE 14-3**

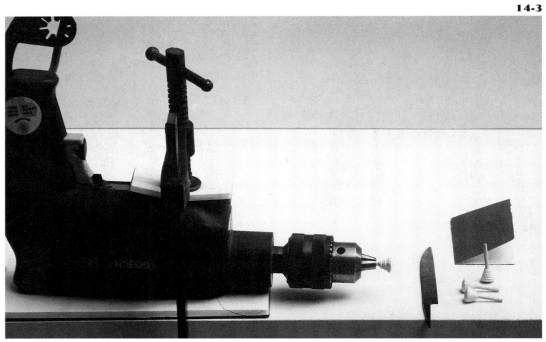

Coat-tree: We used a portable drill clamped to a work surface, file, and abrasive paper as lathe, and tools for making the balsa cones.

14-4

FIGURE 14-4

Coat-tree: The balsa cones, hardwood dowels, and aluminum tubes.

FIGURES 14-5, 14-6, 14-7

Wooden chair system; designed by the authors, 1985; project; 1:3 scale model.

A further variation of the project shown in Figures 13-12, 13-13, 13-14, and 13-15. We made many changes, but the client still did not like our design. In this case, to enable the client to save on equipment expenses, we decided on a metal wire structure as a common element for the whole family of chairs. We also tried to give our design a more traditional look.

The foamcore seats and backrests of the models were covered with fabric or white paper. The legs were made of balsa dowels; the metal frame was made from brass wire bonded with epoxy.

14-6

▼14-5

14-7▶

14-8

Wooden chair system: These 1:4 and 1:5 scale models were made only for checking the structure's design and were never shown to the client. It was an attempt to make the common structural element of the chairs out of tubes and sheet metal.

The models were made with aluminium tubing, aluminum sheets, and iron wire, bonded with epoxy. The 1:5 model (Fig. 14-9 center) was made of iron wire; instead of gluing the two wire parts we soldered them, since there was such a small contact area.

14-9

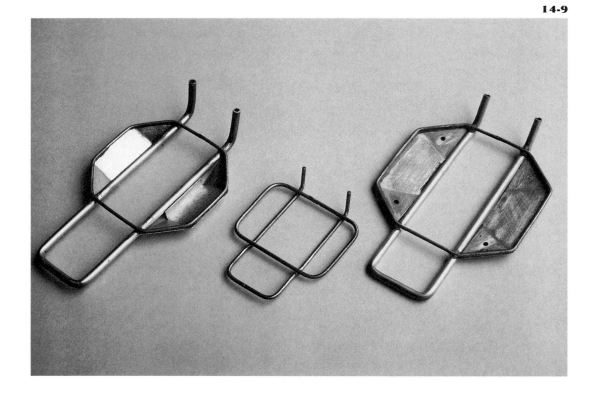

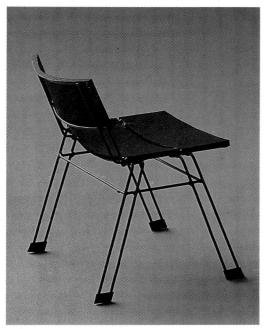

14-10

14-11

Wire stacking chair; designed by the authors, 1980; project.

Figure 14-10 shows a 1:5 scale model made with piano wire and black three-ply paper. The joints were soldered. Figure 14-11 shows the full-size prototype of the metal structure.

FIGURES 14-12, 14-13

Stacking chair, "Tuia"; designed by the authors, 1978; manufactured by T 70, Giussano (Milan), Italy; 1:4 scale model.

The model was made of spruce, piano wire, and canvas; the metal structure was soldered and the canvas hem glued.

14-12

14-13

FIGURE 14-14

Wall-mounted desk and shelving unit; designed by the authors, 1985; project; 1:5 scale model.

This very compact desk is fitted with shelves and accessories. Besides performing the structural job of supporting the shelves, the central steel tube also makes easier the job of mounting the unit to the wall. The tube was designed to contain lamp, computer, and telephone wires.

The model has balsa wood shelves bordered with colored two-ply paper; the foamcore writing desk is covered with colored two-ply paper; drawer and desk accessories are balsa; shelf accessories are piano wire and welded mesh; the central rod is PVC; mounting accessories are laminated paper.

14-14

14-15

14-16

FIGURE 14-15

Kitchen unit, "Brooklyn"; designed by the authors, 1985; manufactured by Aiko, Caldogno (Vicenza), Italy.

This kitchen unit was designed as an alternative to the costly and limiting tradition of wall-to-wall modules; it is a self-contained unit available only in a few simple variations. It is reasonably priced and can be placed in any room with no alignment problems and no wall mounting required. (Photo: Franco Chimenti—Bitetto & Chimenti)

FIGURE 14-16

Kitchen unit, "Brooklyn"; 1:10 scale model.

The model was foamcore covered with white and colored two-ply paper, with piano wire details and balsa posts. Metal-finish paper was used for the sink and cooktop; black glossy paper for the oven door. The electric burners and their knobs were made from black three-ply paper. See the same model with refrigerator and cabinet in Figure 1-51. This model is shown again here because of the strong effect the balsa wood posts have on the design.

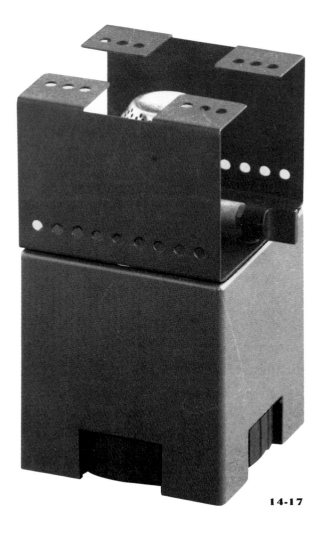

14-17

FIGURE **14-17**

Camping stove, "Kubo"; designed by the authors, 1983; manufactured by Uniflame, Milan, Italy.

The square base gives stability to the unit and allows for the manufacture of stoves with two or more burners. The sheet metal pan support protects the flame from the wind. The gas bottle casing is plastic to prevent condensation.

FIGURE **14-18**

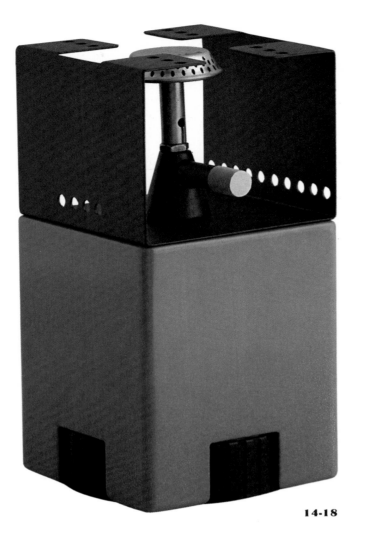

14-18

Camping stove, "Kubo"; full-size model.

The casing was made of balsa sheets (⅛ inch/3mm thick); the big recessed knob at the base for holding the gas bottle was made of black four-ply paper; the sheet-metal stand for holding the pan was made of $\frac{3}{64}$ inch-thick (1mm) aluminum sheet; the cone at the base of the burner was made of a block of balsa wood; the gas knob was made of colored two-ply paper.

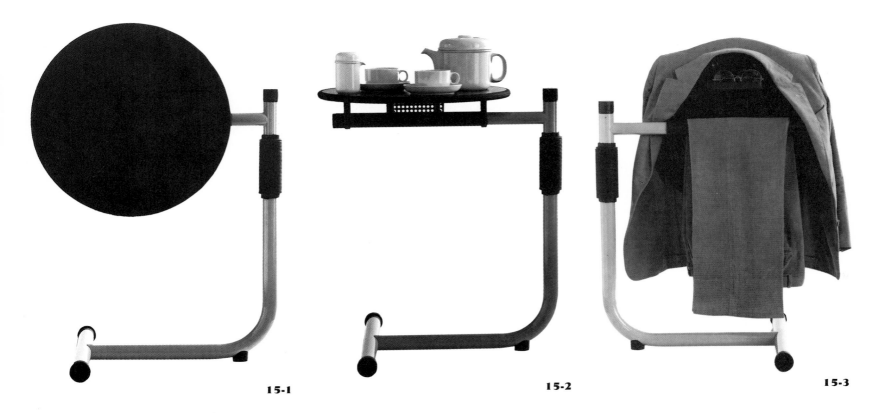

15-1 15-2 15-3

FIGURES 15-1, 15-2, 15-3

Table-cart, "Trio"; designed by the authors, 1979; manufactured by Magis, Motta di Livenza (Treviso), Italy.

"Trio" is a multifunctional object: It can be used as a service table in the bedroom, for eating and reading; and as a bedroom valet stand. The top can be raised and tilted.

This small table turned out to be very successful, a winner of design prizes and an item in the design collections of the Museums of Contemporary Arts in Chicago and Paris.

15-4

15-5 ▶

FIGURE 15-4

Table-cart, "Trio"; 1:5 scale model.

The frame was built with a bent PVC dowel; the wheel axle was glued to the stand with PVC glue; the wheels were from a toy; the top was made of balsa wood and was bordered with black two-ply paper.

15-6

15-7

Chair; designed by the authors, 1988; manufactured by Alacta, Meda (Milan), Italy; 1:4 scale model.

This metal chair has interchangeable parts. The seat can be upholstered or made of perforated metal or plywood. There are versions with and without arms.

Figure 15-6 shows the materials of the different versions: at center, perforated metal (in the model we used a found object, expanded steel mesh cut from a heatproof-glass pot flame protector); in the lower right corner, painted plywood (in the model we used black laminated four-ply paper); at center right, upholstery (in the model we used lightweight black cotton). Figure 15-7 shows the upholstered version with and without arms.

The 1:4 scale model was made with PVC dowels of different sizes, painted black and silver. Vinyl electrical wire insulation was used to make the black sleeve that covers the arm.

FIGURE **15-8**

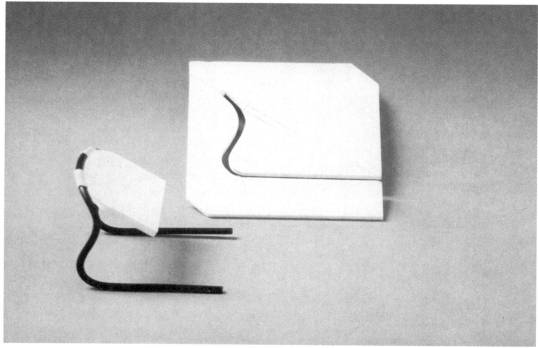

Chair; 1:4 scale model: Foamcore molds were used to bend the PVC dowel for the seat structure.

FIGURE 15-9

Chair; 1:4 scale model: Holes were made in the large-diameter PVC dowel at the points where the legs and seat structure were fixed. The legs and the seat structure dowels were plugged into these holes and then glued with PVC glue.

15-8

15-9

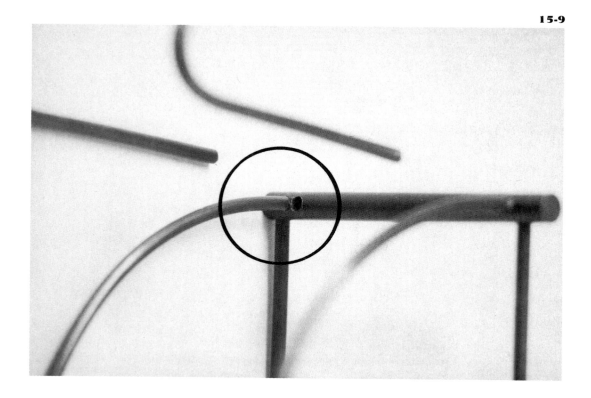

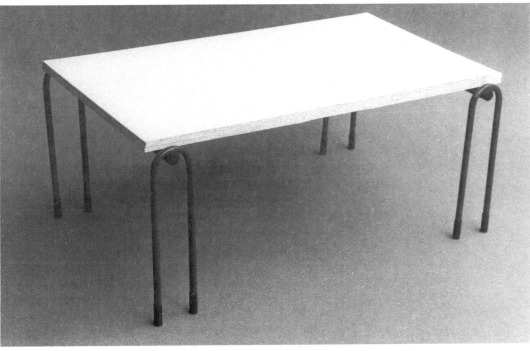

15-10

FIGURE **15-10, 15-11**

Table; designed by the authors, 1982; project; 1:5 scale model.

The legs were made with PVC dowels; the longitudinal beams were hardwood sticks epoxied to the rest of the structure and painted; the top was laminated from four sheets of very heavy Bristol board ($^{1}/_{16}$ inch/1.6mm thick).

15-11

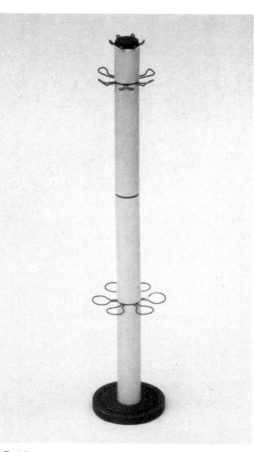

15-12

Collapsible coat-tree; designed by the authors, 1987; project; 1:6 scale model.

The idea was to design a very low-priced coat-tree made of a PVC tube (5-inch/125mm PVC drain) and steel wire. The object could be easily assembled at home without tools simply by plugging in the pieces.

The model was also made of PVC tubing; the plugs were balsa wood dowels covered with black paper; the accessories were made of iron wire and the base of black four-ply paper. The disassembled model can be seen in Figure 10-8.

15-13

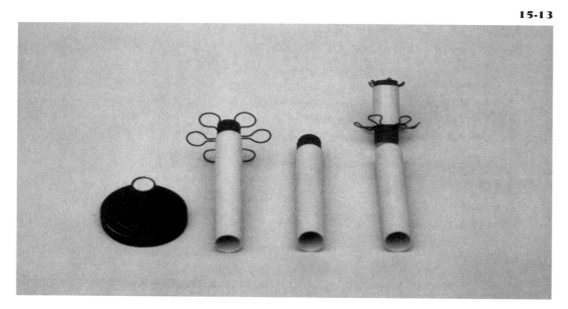

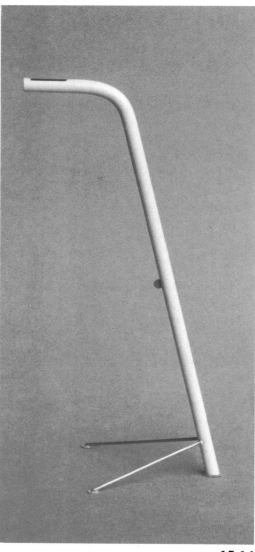

15-14

FIGURE 15-14

Floor-standing uplight, "Liana"; designed by the authors, 1982; manufactured by Valenti, Milan, Italy; 1:10 scale model.

In this model we used PVC rod for the main body of the lamp, iron wire for the legs, and colored three-ply paper for the details.

FIGURE **15-15**

Eyeglass frames; designed by the authors, 1985; project; 1:1 scale model.

We used existing eyewires but transformed their sections using files and abrasive paper; the temple was made from a polystyrene dowel. The end piece and bridge were cut out from a sheet of polystyrene, as were the nose pads, to which colored two-ply paper was added to give the feeling of colored rubber.

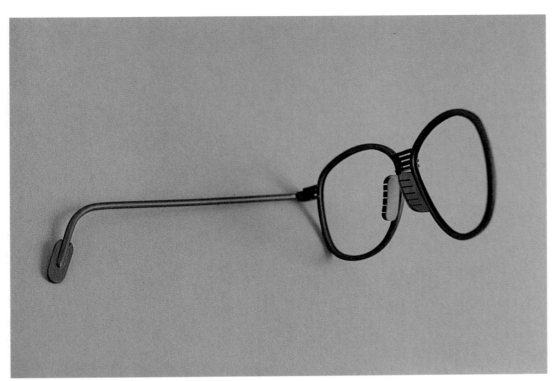

15-15

FIGURE **15-16**

15-16

Eyeglass frames; designed by the authors, 1985; project; 1:1 scale model.

Again we used existing eyewires, altering their shape with files and abrasive paper. The hinge and end piece were made of a polystyrene dowel that had been worked with a small file to create a corrugated tube effect. The temple was made with piano wire. The nose pads came from the existing frame, but fringes were cut into them and the cuts filled in with narrow strips of colored three-ply paper.

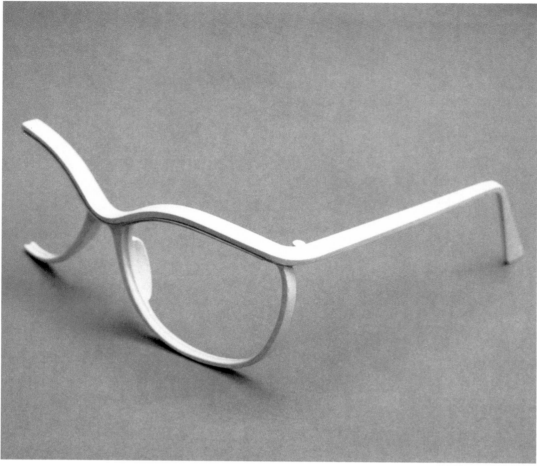

15-17

FIGURE **15-17**

Eyeglass frames; designed by the authors, 1985; project; 1:1 scale model.

The eyewires came from existing frames; the upper part was substituted with a polystyrene strip, heat-shaped expressly for this design. A narrow strip of colored paper interposed between the existing and newly designed parts makes an interesting aesthetic detail.

FIGURE **15-18**

Kitchen scales; designed by the authors, 1980; project; full-size models.

These paper models (colored three-ply paper and black four-ply paper) were made following the technique described in Pre-shaping Wide Radiuses, Chapter 1.

The graduated cups, which function also as coverings for the scales, were made with clear acetate sheets $\frac{1}{32}$ inch (0.8mm) thick; clear polyester tape was used for bonding the acetate. The graphics were made with dry transfer lettering and the lines with charting tape.

15-18

16-1

FIGURE 16-1

Sofa; designed by the authors, 1981; project; 1:10 scale models.

This is a basic modular seating system for waiting rooms, hotel halls, and other public spaces; conceptually it was a simple table with cushions. The backrest was unconventional but suited to a sofa for public spaces; it was made from rubber cords, such as those used for tying luggage to car roof racks.

The models were made of $\frac{3}{16}$-inch (5mm) balsa sheets, hardwood dowels, rubber bands, lightweight cotton, and polyester batting.

FIGURES 16-2, 16-3

16-2

Lounge chair; designed by the authors, 1984; project; 1:5 scale model.

This collapsible lounge chair was developed to be sold in department stores. The project called for the economy of costs and materials.

In the model the cushion was upholstered with cotton shirt fabric and stuffed with polyester batting. The seat support and backrest were made of plastic screening. In the real product it would have been made out of nylon woven mesh. The braces (Fig. 16-3, top right) were made of ⅛-inch-thick (3mm) aluminum wire and held in place by the black pockets (two-ply paper) glued on the seat support screening. The base was made of balsa wood; the geometric texture on the base was made with a very narrow file.

16-3

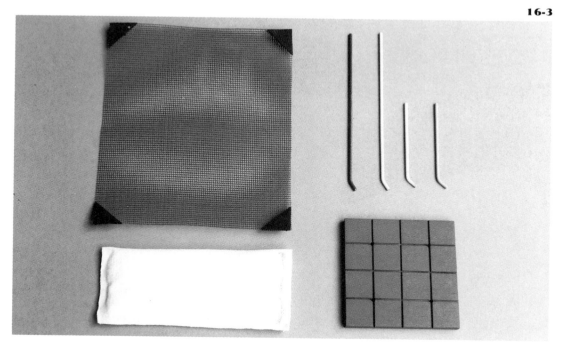

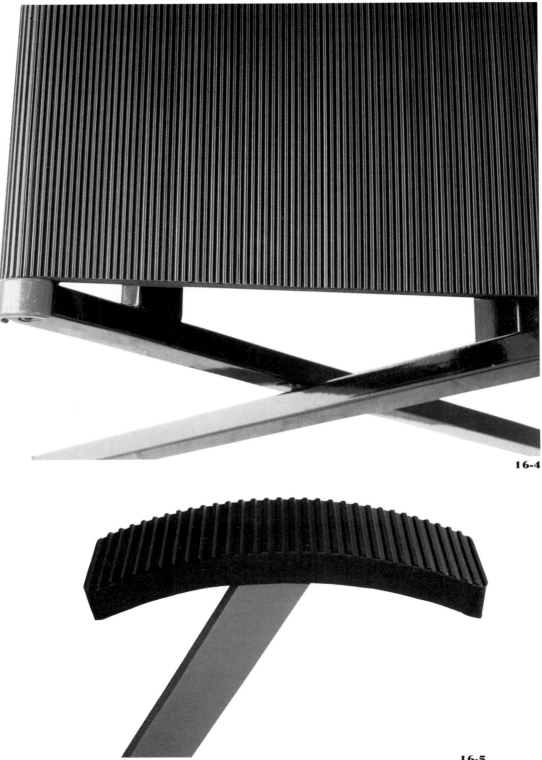

FIGURE 16-4

Folding chair, "Margherita"; designed by the authors, 1988; manufactured by Elam, Meda (Milan), Italy; 1:1 scale model.

Detail of the model's seat surface, showing the use of textured rubber: The same detail with a different texture is shown in Figure 1-54; in the real product the texture is similar to the one pictured in Figure 1-54.

FIGURE 16-5

Chair arm; designed by the authors, 1987; project; 1:1 scale model.

Textured rubber was used for the top surface of the model chair arm. The rubber was glued to a structure that resembled a box lid, built out of black four-ply paper; the entire assemblage was supported by a brace made of two strips of foamcore covered with colored two-ply paper.

16-4

16-5

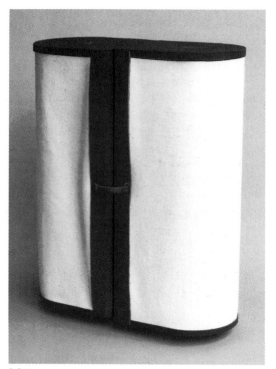

16-6

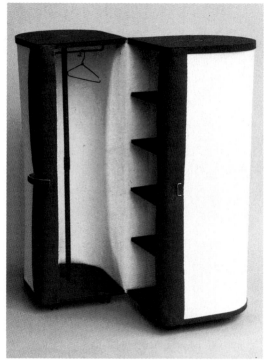

16-7

FIGURES 16-6, 16-7, 16-8

Movable folding wardrobe; designed by the authors, 1988; project; 1:5 scale model.

The concept was to create a light-weight wardrobe that was similar to a garment bag. The model was made of heavy-duty canvas, trimmed in leather and kept in position and under tension by black painted aluminum poles, as the real product would have been. The shelves and the top and bottom trays were made of black laminated three-ply paper. The poles were attached to the trays with screws.

Note the leather handle, made in the way traditional suitcases' handles used to be.

Figure 16-8 shows all of the wardrobe's parts. The product would have been sold as a kit to be assembled at home.

16-8

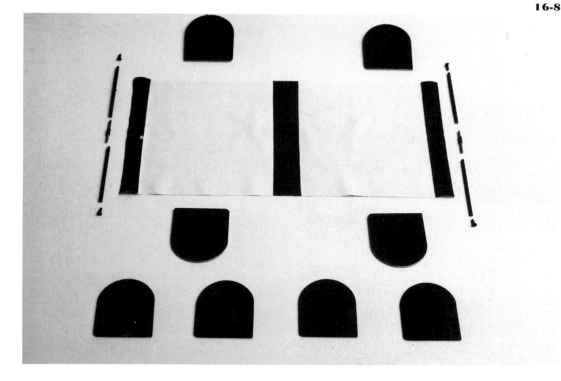

16-9

Pram, collapsible rowboat; designed by the authors, 1985; project.

We designed and built this 7-foot-long (2.15m) pram as a tender to "White Artemide," the sailing catamaran shown in Figures 13-34 and 13-35. The small pram was made of marine plywood and PVC-coated fabric, the type used for inflatable rafts.

16-10

FIGURES 16-11, 16-12

Pram, collapsible rowboat; 1:10 scale models.

There were two different options for folding the boat: in one the bulkheads were removable; in the other the bulkheads folded in half. The models were made of cotton shirt fabric and balsa wood, held together with fabric hinges.

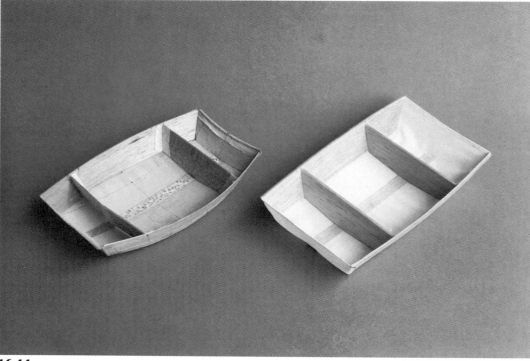

16-11

16-12

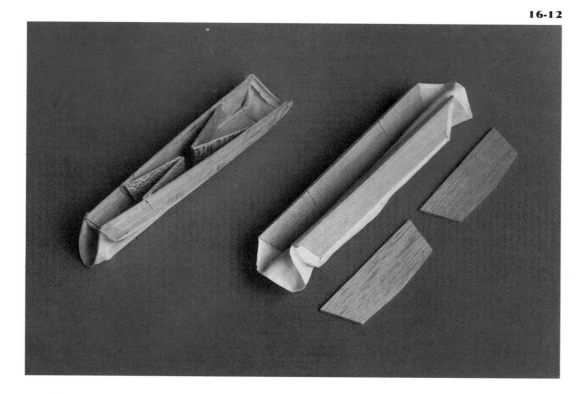

EXAMPLES

17-1

FIGURE 17-1

Exhibition, "The Artist's House"; designed by Roberto Lucci, Paolo Orlandini, Federica Zanuso, 1983; organized by Triennale di Milano; sponsored by CARIPLO, Milan, Italy.

The title of this project was "The Artist's House"; it was created for the exhibition Le Case della Triennale, held in Milan and Paris in 1983. We explored the theme of the *casa* (house) in an abstract way, utilizing the exhibition space for showing design examples. The assumption was that the designer can be considered the artist of the industrial society. The objects shown were not taken from the production line but were either prototypes or reinterpretations of existing products.

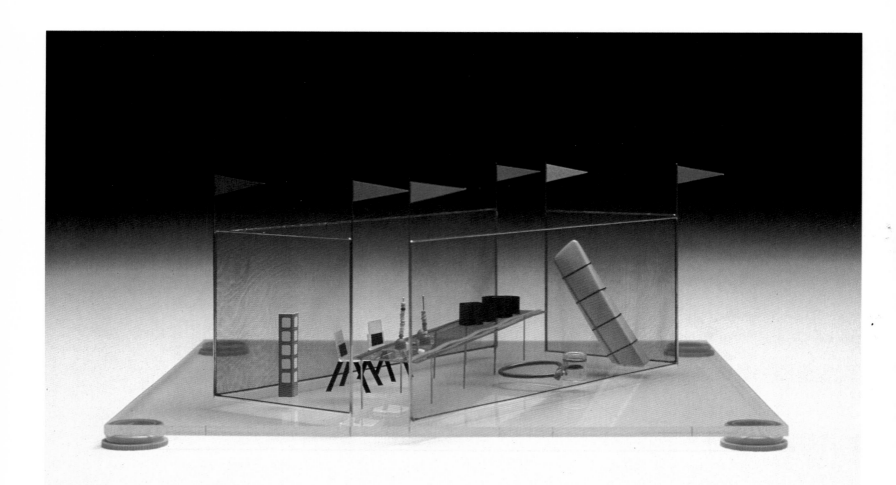

17-2

FIGURE 17-2

Exhibition, "The Artist's House"; 1:20 scale model.

Since the exhibition was filled with products, it made sense to use found objects as a small-scale reinterpretation of the real product world.

We used a sheet of clear polymethylmethacrylate for the base, and pill bottle caps for the feet; tulle fabric stretched on frames of ⁵⁄₆₄-inch (2mm) brass tubing for the walls (mosquito screening and window frames in the real exhibition stand). Paper was used for the flags and the TV sets; a paper brochure was used for the folding ladder (see Figs. 11-33 to 11-36).

The chairs and table were made from acetate sheet; the legs were wooden sticks and piano wire. Colored beads and clear plastic caps were used for the other objects. The catamaran hull was a piece of a scale model.

17-3

17-4

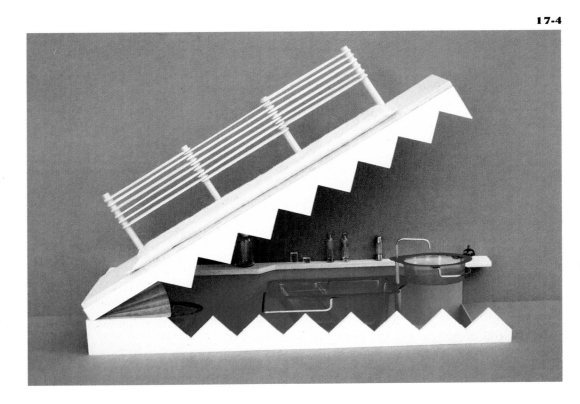

Exhibition, "Bathroom-Living Room"; designed by the authors, 1988; organized by the Italian Trade Institute, Düsseldorf, W. Germany; 1:10 scale model.

Since the project was made for an exhibition, it was far from being a practical thing; on the contrary, it was the caricature of a concept that could also be reinterpreted in a more serious way. The idea was to show a sofa that opened into a bathroom.

The sofa was derived from an old project of ours (see Fig. 16-1). At the base of the sofa we added a foamcore panel that divided into two parts and suggested the ideas of both a dust ruffle and alligator teeth. The alligator's mouth opened to disclose a bathroom.

The bathroom appliances were made from blister packaging (Fig. 17-5). We sprayed the clear blister shapes with a very light coat of paint. Faucets and towel racks were made of zinc-coated iron wire; bottles on a foamcore shelf were obtained from old electrical fuses.

The opening and closing movement of the alligator mouth was provided by a battery-operated electric motor taken from a toy. The motor and the battery were located in the back of the background panel.

17-5

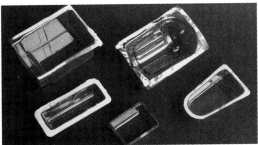

17-6

FIGURE 17-6

Winter holiday capsule; designed by the authors, 1970; project; 1:20 scale model.

This winter vacation shelter was collapsible and transportable. It resembles an LEM (lunar landing module), inspired by the first manned Moon landing, which had occurred just one year earlier. It was meant to be a do-it-yourself kit made from various readily available consumer items (polyethylene bowls, garbage pail lids, aluminum tubing, aluminum-coated polyester film, expanded polyethylene).

The model was a real collection of found objects, from pill bottle caps and Christmas tree balls to map tacks and children's toy parts. The model's skin, like in the real project, was made from polyester film but the aluminum coating was imitated with aluminum adhesive foil.

17-7

FIGURE 17-7

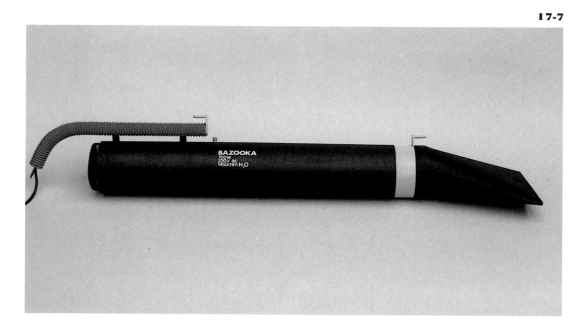

Vacuum cleaner; designed by the authors, 1979; project; 1:1 scale model.

Our aim was to design a lightweight but sturdy vacuum cleaner that could be produced without the need for a heavy investment in molds.

The body of the real product would have been made of a 5-inch (125mm) PVC tube. Minor complementary parts and accessories would have completed the unit.

To some extent, the model was made like the real product would have been made. We used PVC drain tube for the main part; the handle was a corrugated electrical wire sleeve stiffened by inserting thick twisted iron. The nozzle was made of black three-ply paper with internal bulkheads (see Working with Paper, Chapter 1). The tail grille was built out of metal screening, as described in Drawing, Chapter 4. The hooks were built out of hardwood.

FIGURE 17-8

17-8

Electronic horoscope; designed by the authors, 1982; project; 1:1 scale model.

The model was built of foamcore covered with glossy black two-ply paper. The keyboard was made with transfer lettering on white paper; the graphics were then reproduced, photographically reversed (to read white on black), printed on photographic paper, and colored with markers (see also Figs. 11-53, 11-62, 11-63).

The design is strongly characterized by the two hemispheres on top of the keyboard. The big one (a Christmas tree decoration) is a cover for the electroluminescent display; the small one (a marble colored with a black marker and trimmed with a white adhesive foil strip at the center) is the on/off switch.

17-9

17-10

Three-wheel vehicle, "Square Meter"; designed by the authors, 1974; project; 1:1 scale model.

This project was made at the time of the first oil crisis, when severe gasoline restrictions were adopted by most countries. We aimed at designing a comfortable small vehicle to be used by everybody (from the young to the old) with many practical features (easy access, maneuverability, room for luggage, optional foul-weather protection).

The model had a plywood body and was fitted with many details that added realism. The handgrips, taillights, headlight, and corrugated tube at the base of the head tube were taken from old motorcycles. The rubber bumpers are tube caps from metal furniture. The fuel tank cap was taken from a plastic bottle for chemicals. The tubes are metal, the chrome finish achieved with aluminum adhesive foil. The hand brake, kick starter, and brake levers are PVC dowels (Bending a Dowel, Chapter 5). The seat was made of rigid polyurethane foam.

The optional foul-weather hood (Fig. 17-10) was made with a glass reinforced polyester sheet; the window was made of transparent PVC; the window gasket is black adhesive tape.

FIGURE **17-11**

Table lamp, "Torcia"; designed by Marili Brandao—third-year student, academic year 1981–82; Industrial Design Department, Istituto Europeo di Design, Milan, Italy; Roberto Lucci and Paolo Orlandini, instructors; Riccardo Zarino, assistant; sponsor: Artemide, Milan, Italy; 1:1 scale prototype.

This and the following lamp (Fig. 17-12) were working prototypes, not just models. They owe their innovative design to the creative use of found objects. The lampstand was made with a toilet tissue tube covered with textured rubber; the lampshade was made with two plastic picnic dishes, a white rubber gasket, and a paper clamp. The lamp uses a 25-watt circular fluorescent bulb. (Photo: Carlo Scillieri)

17-11

FIGURE **17-12**

Desk lamp, "Pollicino"; designed by Marina Clerici—third-year student, academic year 1981–82; Industrial Design Department, Istituto Europeo di Design, Milan; Roberto Lucci and Paolo Orlandini, instructors; Riccardo Zarino, assistant; sponsor: Artemide, Milan, Italy. 1:1 scale prototype.

The lamp base was made from a dry sponge and was weighed down by an electrical transformer inside it. The movable arm was made from an aluminum tube and the base articulation created from a Ping-Pong ball painted black. The reflector is an old aluminum pill tube, cut and reassembled with epoxy glue. The lamp uses a 20-watt halogen bulb. (Photo: Carlo Scillieri)

17-12

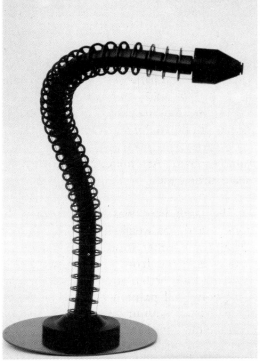

17-13

Bionic robot arm, "Naturo Due"; designed by Carlo Bombardelli, Paolo Bodega, Emanuele De Dominicis; Centro Ricerche Strutture Naturali, Istituto Europeo di Design, Milan, Italy 1983; with the collaboration of the CSI Workshop of Montedipe, Bollate (Milan), Italy; Italtel Telematica, Milan, Italy; Ranger Italiana, Carate Brianza (Milan), Italy.

The main features of "Naturo Due" are its high degrees of flexibility and agility; the innovative design was derived from studying the muscles in an elephant's trunk and the spinal columns of fish.

The working model shown in Figure 17-14 was made with plastic balls and nylon twine. The working prototype is shown in Figure 17-13; a fiberoptic eye is mounted on the movable end of the arm. It was exhibited in 1985 at the seventeenth Triennale di Milano, Italy, and in 1986 at the Centre Pompidou in Paris, France.

17-14

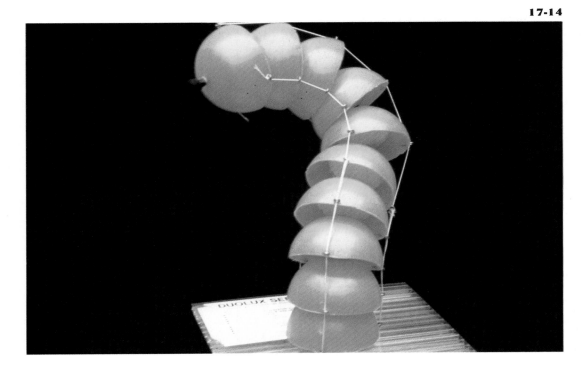

17-15

17-16

FIGURES 17-15, 17-16, 17-17

Sailboat reproductions, 1980; 1:50 scale models.

The three photos show reproductions of traditional Samoan (Fig. 17-15), Kenyan (Fig. 17-16), and Brazilian (Fig. 17-17) sailboats.

The interesting feature of these models is that they were made entirely with found materials. The small wooden sticks were found on the beach already worked and polished by sand and sea. The sails are scraps of fabric also found on the beach. The only added material was rope, used for the rigging and for holding together the boats, as in traditional boats.

Note the details in Figure 17-15: The anchor was made with a stone and the Polynesian sextant was made with tiny wooden sticks.

Although these models do not represent a new design, we thought they were worth showing in this book. Not only are they good examples of how to make models with found objects, but they symbolize our model-making philosophy: They are refined models made with the minimum of material and equipment.

17-17

Index